W9-BCV-965

SEP 2 7 2011
10-18(9)

COCKTAIL HOUR
UNDER THE TREE
OF FORGETFULNESS

COCKTAIL HOUR UNDER THE TREE OF FORGETFULNESS

ALEXANDRA FULLER

THORNDIKE
WINDSOR
PARAGON

This Large Print edition is published by Thorndike Press, Waterville, Maine USA and by AudioGo Ltd, Bath, England.
Copyright© Alexandra Fuller, 2011.
The moral right of the author has been asserted.
Photographs on pages 301, 327, 332, and 345 by Ian Murphy. Other photographs courtesy of the author and her family.
Pages 355–358 constitute an extension of this copyright page.
Map illustration by Jeffrey L. Ward.
Thorndike Press, a part of Gale, Cengage Learning.

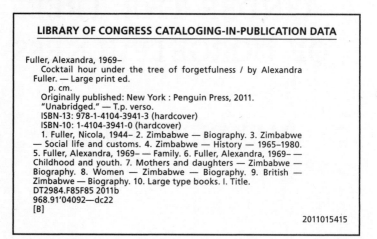

LIBRARY OF CONGRESS CATALOGING-IN-PUBLICATION DATA

Fuller, Alexandra, 1969–
    Cocktail hour under the tree of forgetfulness / by Alexandra Fuller. — Large print ed.
        p. cm.
    Originally published: New York : Penguin Press, 2011.
    "Unabridged." — T.p. verso.
    ISBN-13: 978-1-4104-3941-3 (hardcover)
    ISBN-10: 1-4104-3941-0 (hardcover)
    1. Fuller, Nicola, 1944– 2. Zimbabwe — Biography. 3. Zimbabwe — Social life and customs. 4. Zimbabwe — History — 1965–1980. 5. Fuller, Alexandra, 1969– — Family. 6. Fuller, Alexandra, 1969– — Childhood and youth. 7. Mothers and daughters — Zimbabwe — Biography. 8. Women — Zimbabwe — Biography. 9. British — Zimbabwe — Biography. 10. Large type books. I. Title.
    DT2984.F85F85 2011b
    968.91'04092—dc22
    [B]
                                                    2011015415

BRITISH LIBRARY CATALOGUING-IN-PUBLICATION DATA AVAILABLE

Published in the U.S. in 2011 by arrangement with The Penguin Press, a member of Penguin Group (USA), Inc.
Published in the U.K. in 2012 by arrangement with Simon & Schuster (UK) Limited.
U.K. Hardcover: 978 1 445 85920 0 (Windsor Large Print)
U.K. Softcover: 978 1 445 85921 7 (Paragon Large Print)

Printed in the United States of America
1 2 3 4 5 6 7 15 14 13 12 11

For Charlie—guide extraordinaire—
with my love

CONTENTS

7

8

CAST OF MAIN CHARACTERS

Nicola Christine Victoria Fuller née Huntingford — the author's mother, also known as Nicola Fuller of Central Africa, Mum or Tub

Timothy Donald Fuller — the author's father, also known as Dad

Vanessa Margaret Fuller — the author's sister, also known as Van

Edith Margaret Belfinley Huntingford née Macdonald — the author's maternal grandmother, also known as Granny or Donnie or Mrs. Huntingford

Roger Lowther Huntingford — the author's maternal grandfather, also known as Hodge

Glennis Duthie — the author's maternal aunt, also known as Auntie Glug or Glug

Sandy Duthie — the author's maternal uncle by marriage

Donald Hamilton Connell-Fuller — the author's paternal grandfather

Ruth Henrietta Fuller — the author's paternal grandmother, also known as Boofy

Tony Fuller — the author's paternal uncle, also known as Uncle Toe

Alexandra Fuller — the author, also known as Bo or Bobo

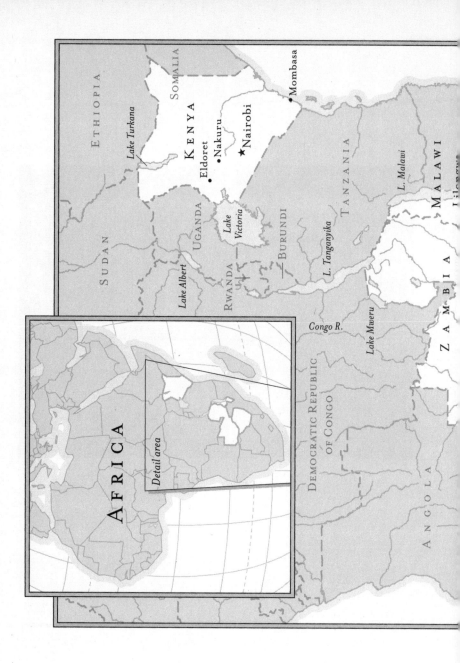

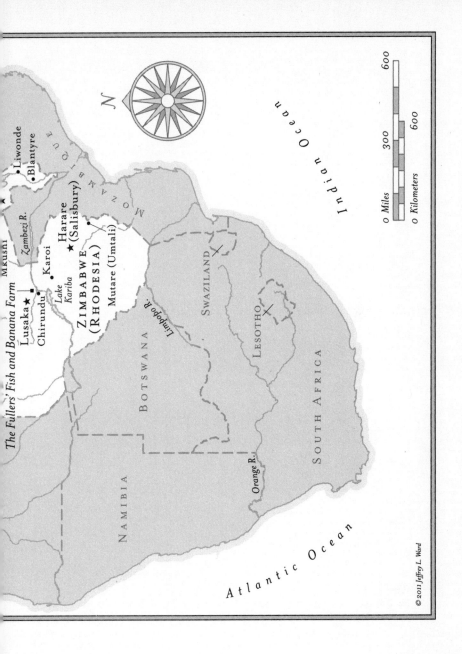

The Fullers Fish and Banana Farm

Liwonde
Blantyre

MOZAMBIQUE

Mkushi

Zambezi R.

Harare
(Salisbury)

Karoi

Lusaka
Chirundu

Lake
Kariba

ZIMBABWE
(RHODESIA)

Mutare (Umtali)

N

Indian Ocean

SWAZILAND

Limpopo R.

BOTSWANA

LESOTHO

SOUTH AFRICA

NAMIBIA

Orange R.

Atlantic Ocean

0 Miles   300   600

0 Kilometers   600

© 2011 Jeffrey L. Ward

PART ONE

The mind I love must have wild places, a tangled orchard where dark damsons drop in heavy grass, an overgrown little wood, the chance of a snake or two, a pool that nobody's fathomed the depth of, and paths threaded with flowers planted by the mind.

— KATHERINE MANSFIELD

NICOLA FULLER OF CENTRAL AFRICA LEARNS TO FLY

Mkushi, Zambia, circa 1986

Mum in an Eldoret theatrical production. Kenya, circa 1963.

Our Mum — or Nicola Fuller of Central Africa, as she has on occasion preferred to introduce herself — has wanted a writer in the

17

family as long as either of us can remember, not only because she loves books and has therefore always wanted to appear in them (the way she likes large, expensive hats, and likes to appear in *them*) but also because she has always wanted to live a fabulously romantic life for which she needed a reasonably pliable witness as scribe.

"At least she didn't read you Shakespeare in the womb," my sister says. "I think that's what gave me brain damage."

"You do not have brain damage," I say.

"That's what Mum says."

"Well, I wouldn't listen to her. You know what she's like," I say.

"I know," Vanessa says.

"For example," I say, "lately, she's been telling me that I must have been switched at birth."

"Really?" Vanessa tilts her head this way and that to get a better view of my features. "Let me have a look at your nose from the other side."

"Stop it," I cover my nose.

"Well, you brought it on yourself," Vanessa says, lighting a cigarette. "You should never have written that Awful Book about her."

I count the ways that Vanessa is wrong, "For the millionth time, it's not awful and it wasn't about her."

Vanessa blows smoke at the sky placidly, "That's not what Mum says. Anyway, I wouldn't know. I haven't read it. I won't. I can't. I'm brain damaged. Ask Mum."

We're sitting outside Vanessa's rock house near the town of Kafue. Wisely, Vanessa has grown up to be an inscrutable artist — fabric, graphics and exuberant, tropical canvases all expressed with a kind of non-committal chaos — so no one can really pin anything on her. And anyway, no matter what happens, Vanessa always behaves as if everything will resolve itself in time as long as no one panics. Her bathroom, for example, has a tree growing through the middle of its thatched roof — very romantic and picturesque but a pitiful defense against rain and reptiles. Vanessa says vaguely, "Oh, just keep your shoes on and have a good look before you sit anywhere and you should be all right."

The rest of the house, attached to the wildly impractical bathroom, has a total of three tiny rooms for Vanessa, her husband and their several children, but it is built on the summit of a kopje, so it has a sense of possibility, like a closet with cathedral ceilings. We sit outside where the air smells of miombo woodland and we smoke cigarettes and look at the comforting lights from the

19

scores of cooking fires smoldering from the kitchens in the surrounding village. Occasionally we hear a dog barking from the taverns on the Kafue Road and soldiers in the nearby army camp shouting to one another or letting off the odd stray bullet. It's all very peaceful.

"Have another glass of wine," Vanessa suggests by way of comforting me. "You never know, Mum might forgive you eventually."

In my defense, the Awful Book, whose full and proper title can never be mentioned in the company of my family, was not all my fault. I had felt more than a little encouraged to write it — directed, even — by Nicola Fuller of Central Africa herself. Having given up on my older sister as a potential writer on account of Vanessa's stubborn refusal to learn how to read or write, Mum settled her literary ambitions on me. I was five when she abandoned the arithmetic section of our weekly Rhodesia Correspondence School packet. "Look Bobo," she reasoned, "numbers are boring. Anyway, you can always pay someone to count for you, but you can never pay anyone to write for you. Now," Mum paused and gave me one of her terrifying smiles. "What do you think you're going to write about?" Then she took a long sip of tea, brushed a couple of dogs off her lap and began to live a life Worthy of Fabulous Literature.

Twelve years later, Mum reviewed her life and matched it up against the kind of biography she hoped to inspire, something along the lines of *West with the Night, The Flame Trees of Thika* or *Out of Africa*. On the whole, she was satisfied. In fact, all things considered, she felt as if she even may have overdone it in some areas (tragedies, war and poverty, for example). However, there remained one glaring omission from her portfolio: there had been no airplanes, and airplanes had featured prominently in the lives of Mum's literary role models.

"And then, as if by magic," Mum says, "My Dashing Little Sri Lankan appeared."

My Dashing Little Sri Lankan did not really belong to Mum — although there were whole moments in the course of her relationship with him when you could have been forgiven for thinking exactly that — and there was debate in the family, some of it quite vigorous, as to whether or not he was dashing, but we could all agree that the Sri Lankan was definitely little. His real name was Mr. Vaas and he said he had come to Zambia to escape all the pain and violence of his native land.

"Then you should feel quite at home with

us," Dad said, which made Mr. Vaas look at him sharply. But my father said nothing more, returning his attention calmly to *Farmers Weekly*. On the whole, I took my father's side. "As usual," Mum said.

"Didn't the last pilot who stayed with us fly his plane into an electricity pole?" I asked, pouring myself another cup of tea.

Without looking up from his magazine, my father said, "I'm afraid so."

Mr. Vaas wilted somewhat.

"Don't listen to them," Mum said, steering Mr. Vaas firmly away from the veranda and tilting him across her garden — an encouraged tangle of bougainvillea and passion fruit vines, beds of lilies and strelitzia, rows of lilac bushes and caladiums looming over borders of impatiens. Mum's current assortment of dogs gamboled at their heels. "My family bullies me terribly," she said. Mr. Vaas patted her arm tactfully, for which the little man was rewarded with a voracious smile. "You and I," Mum foretold, "will show them all what real courage looks like. We will be the Blixen and Finch Hatton of Zambia."

Mr. Vaas blinked an SOS back at me and Dad from the gloaming.

"How's that tea, Bobo?" Dad asked. "Still hot?"

"Scorching," I said.

■ ■ ■ ■

Now faded Mr. Vaas, then Mum, into the home paddock, where the dairy cattle had come into the open to shelter from the evening mosquitoes. "Come fly with me," I could hear Mum sing, "let's fly, let's fly away. If you can use some exotic booze, there's a bar in far Bombay. Come fly with me, let's fly, let's fly away."

Dad is quite deaf as a result of hearing too many guns go off during the course of his life, not all of them fired by Mum, so he could not hear Nicola Fuller of Central Africa but I felt it was only fair to warn him that Sinatra had entered into the picture. Dad put down his magazine. "Well, good luck to the little Indian," he said.

"Sri Lankan," I corrected him.

Dad lit a cigarette.

"Come fly with me," Mum serenaded — now her voice seemed to be drifting to us from the direction of the tobacco barns — "let's float down to Peru."

So, encouraged by Mum's almost aggressive enthusiasm, Mr. Vaas parked his elderly and very basic Cessna on the airstrip by the Mkushi Country Club (whose tennis courts had ruptured little trees and which housed bats in the bar) and declared himself open

23

for business as a flight instructor. Because no one dies in this story, and death tends to sharpen the memory, I can't now remember who else attended the flying course, but there must have been one or two other farmers and perhaps a couple of farmers' wives. Anyway, as in almost any story that includes Mum, they are beside the point.

Mum took to flying "like a bird to the wing," she sang, although she had some difficulty with the paperwork required to ensure a reasonably uneventful journey. "Numbers," she confided, darkly. "I suppose I should have paid more attention when those bloody nuns were trying to teach me how to count." Navigation and fuel loads, for example, she found "very confusing." Still, a minor detail like her complete inability to count further than the ten fingers on her two hands did nothing to dissuade either Mum or Mr. Vaas from pursuing her dream of taking to the air all through the smoky haze of that winter and into the first burning days of spring.

The late October afternoon on which Mum scheduled her first attempts to take off and land coincided with a full moon. Mum and Mr. Vaas took the creaking Cessna down to the end of the airstrip, its wings juddering in the settling heat of the long day. She turned it into the wind and faced the rising hunter's moon, blood red in a smoke-stained sky. Mr. Vaas talked Mum through a final instrument check and from the tiny, greasy cockpit window, she looked back at the little tin hut in which the other flying students waited and gave the world her final thumbs-up.

The plane rattled down the runway, hopping old antbear holes and kicking up red dust. It gave one or two little jumps, and then it soared upward, tipping this way and that, before clearing the tops of the msasa trees, their new spring leaves paradoxically orange, red and yellow. Mr. Vaas looked over at Mum. "How are we doing, Mrs. Fuller?"

For those other students listening in the little tin hut next to the runway, there was a crackly moment and then came the voice of Nicola Fuller of Central Africa, shaking a little with all the uncommon, crazy courage that enabled Mum to see adventure and possibility where others saw only disaster and tragedy. "Fly me to the moon," came her voice, singing not very steady but clear enough, "let me play among the stars."

There was a pause. Mum looked over at Mr. Vaas and smiled alarmingly. His forehead had broken out in little beads of sweat. "And it takes quite a lot to make a Sri Lankan sweat," she said afterward.

"Take it easy," Mr. Vaas said.

Mum's voice came over the radio again, stronger now, "Let me see what spring is like on Jupiter and Mars."

As the little plane climbed and climbed toward the dropping sun, a brave punctuation of dark purple in a vivid red sky, Mr. Vaas gesticulated wildly. "Go back to land, go back to land!"

Mum wanted to fly over the aerial gun stationed on the Mkushi River Bridge. The Rhodesians had blown up this bridge during the Rhodesian Bush War, which seems excessive, even in hindsight, given that the bridge was at least a day or two's drive from the Rhodesian front lines (roads being what they were). Then, in belated and approximate retaliation (the war having ended), the Zambian army had set up a permanent gunner on the north side of the bridge against the South African Defense Forces. In view of the fact that South Africa is a quarter of a continent away and the real fighting was taking place elsewhere as usual, the Zambian gunners didn't have much to shoot at. Out of sheer boredom, they'd been known to take beer-fueled potshots at anything within reasonable range: crows, eucalyptus trees, chickens. There was no saying what they would do when faced with an actual unscheduled flight of an honest-to-goodness airplane.

Mr. Vaas became very firm. "I don't have clearance for the bridge. Take her back down to the ground."

"In other words," Mum sang, "hold my hand."

Mr. Vaas glared at her. "We land. We take off. We land. We take off. Bump. *Bump*. Bump. *Bump*. No bridges and no singing, for God's sake."

Mum looked at My Little Sri Lankan with sorrowful reproach. "We could go to Zaire," she offered. "It's just over those little hills."

Mr. Vaas glared more and more fiercely. "Time to return to earth," he said.

Mum's eyes misted, but she nodded. "Roger," she said. She knew then, she said afterward, that she'd never fly alone — as she had dreamed she might — across the high plateau of Zambia, down the escarpment and up the Luangwa River, elephants fanning out ahead of her, the light thinned by altitude and adrenaline into something approaching the perfect light of her childhood. "I took that little plane down and landed it and said good-bye to one more dream," she said.

In memoriam of her dashed dream, Mum put the three volumes of Trevor Thom's *The Air Pilot's Manual* on her bathroom shelf next to Charles Berlitz's *German Step-by-Step* and Commander F. J. Hewett's *Sailing a Small Boat*. "Well you can't win them all," she says. And with her characteristic, if uneven, gift for magnanimity, she forgave My Dashing Little Sri Lankan, even after it became apparent, at least to her, that he was a spectacularly indifferent flight instructor. "As far as I know, not a single one of us passed even the written portion of the exam," Mum says. But her chin goes up. "In any case, I flew, didn't I? I flew."

And it is true that no one can take away the day when she flew the plane up over the msasa trees, around the country club grounds and back down again onto the airstrip with a sunset at her tail, the bumpy landing into the face of the great, fiery hunter's moon. The propeller spun to a halt. The cockpit door opened. Dust settled. For a moment the whole world stopped breathing. Then, while Mr. Vaas mopped his brow in the copilot's seat, Beryl Markham and

Karen Blixen had nothing on the way Mum emerged smiling from the cockpit, flashing a V for Victoria to her adoring fans, real and imaginary.

NICOLA HUNTINGFORD
IS BORN

Isle of Skye, Scotland, 1944

The stairway in Waternish House. Scotland, circa 1940.

Nicola Fuller of Central Africa holds dear to her heart the values of her clan: loyalty to blood, passion for land, death before surrender. They're the sorts of values that lead you to kill and that get you killed, and in every important way, they were precisely the kind of stubborn tribal values that you needed if you were bound and determined to be White, and stay White, first during Kenya's Mau Mau and later during the Rhodesian War. They were decidedly not the values of the Johnny-come-lately White liberals who survived postindependence in those African countries by declaring with suddenly acquired backbone and conviction that they'd always been on the side of "the people" and that they had always embraced all of humanity and that inequality had always been so hard for them to witness.

"Oh dear," Mum says, pained. "Embracing all of humanity? Must we? Isn't that like born-again Christians?" (Mum has nothing against born-agains, but she has never recovered from the time she accidentally attended an evangelical service in England. "Suddenly there were all these weeping people trying to hold my hand.") "Oh dear," Mum says. "No, I don't think so."

Mum has fought for what she saw as Her Land in Africa, and she fought fiercely and without apology. So it's confusing, but very instructive, to consider her political heroes (you can tell who she admires because she names her pets after them): Che Guevara, Josip Broz Tito and Aung San Suu Kyi. In other words, Mum admires leaders of "the people" while seeming to have absolutely no patience for "the people" themselves. On the other hand, I suppose it is only fair to disclose that she had a cat named Maggie Thatcher and she has named a new Jack Russell puppy Papa Doc. "He's *so* dictatorial," Mum wrote proudly in a recent letter. "He's already taught himself to frown and he's only six weeks old."

Nicola Fuller of Central Africa was born in the front room of the housekeeper's cottage on her mother's family's Waternish Estate on the Isle of Skye on July 9, 1944. Her mother was a Macdonald of Clanranald. The clan member crest badge shows a disembodied arm brandishing a disproportionately massive sword emerging from the top of a castle. The clan motto, which I'm not sure anyone takes too seriously, is "My hope is constant in Thee." The war cry, which I think everyone takes very seriously, is *Dh'aindeoin co theireadhe e,* which translates from the Scottish Gaelic into English as "Gainsay who dare."

It took me a while to recover from the discovery that Mum's family actually had a war cry, but then I thought about Mum and I realized that if you didn't have a war cry to go with that attitude, you'd have to invent one. During the bush war in Rhodesia Mum

forwent her family's Gaelic war cry and took up a personal war cry. It was borrowed from Cliff Richard and the Shadows, and was about being a bandit from Brazil, being the quickest on the trigger and shooting to kill, which was about the extent of Mum's interest in the lyrics. In fact she quite often didn't make it past the opening word — a loudly shouted "Olé!," which kept it simple for everyone who did not speak Gaelic but confused those of us who spoke absolutely no Spanish. Vanessa and I translated the word as "Hooray!" But the meaning was clear either way. My mother was here, she was armed, and you bet your insurrecting Commie ass she was dangerous.

My grandmother named her first child Nicola Christine Victoria — three Christian names to make up for all the children she had miscarried on the way to having this one — Nicola to commemorate a Nichols branch of their family; Christine after the housekeeper on Waternish who helped my grandmother give birth and Victoria because Mum was born a little over a month after D-day.

Including Nicola Christine Victoria, three children were born on Waternish that day, which made it something of a baby boom. What made the other two children memorable and worthy of sharing a headline with

my usually headline-hogging Mum was the fact that one was eventually diagnosed with a form of dwarfism and one was born with her feet on backward. "How lucky," my grandmother is said to have remarked upon hearing the news. "That'll come in handy if she wants to catch razor fish."

"Why razor fish?" I ask.

"Razor fish," Mum explains, "live in the sand along the shore. You sneak up on them by walking backward." .

In spite of living all but a fraction of her life in Africa, Mum considers herself one million percent Highland Scottish, ethnically speaking. Her father was English, but Mum says that doesn't count; Scottish blood (especially the Highland sort) cancels English blood. As if to prove this, Mum cries when bagpipes play; she once attempted to slip a suitcase full of haggis through Zambian customs (to be fair, she was experiencing a manic episode at the time) and her eyes actually change color from green to yellow when she is excited or is about to go certifiably mad. Mum is also a bit fey, which means that she has access to worlds unseen, has funny feelings about things, insights, prophecies and visions. She believes in ghosts and fairies.

She inherited this gift from her two mil-

lion percent Highland Scottish mother, ethnically speaking, who was *so* fey that she could predict the future with astonishing accuracy. "It'll all end in tears, you'll see," my grandmother used to say several times a day. My grandmother could actually talk to fairies and see ghosts with casual ease, especially after her second midmorning gin and French, which became the habit of her later years (but this is also the woman who claimed that the reason she walked in circles after eleven a.m. was that one leg was shorter than the other, so it's hard to know).

I, on the other hand, don't seem to have inherited Mum's passion for violence. I am not fey like my grandmother. I don't make unilateral declarations of independence every time we all have too much to drink. My eyes are dark green and stay that way, no matter how angry or excited I get. I can see that Scotland is beautiful, or that parts of it are, but I don't fall to my knees as soon as I land on the Isle of Skye and begin inhaling the peat. Plus, even though one of my legs is shorter than the other, I very rarely walk in circles, even when drunk.

"Which just goes to show you," Mum says. "You must have been swapped at birth. You're missing that clan loyalty. Fidelity to family above all else. Blood, blood, blood."

To rub it in, she has started introducing me to people as "my *American* daughter." Then she leaves a meaningful pause to let my otherness, my overt over-there-ness sink in, before adding with a mirthless laugh, "Careful what you say or do, or she'll put you in an Awful Book."

In this way, Mum has made it clear that the blood of her ancestors has come to a screeching halt in the blue walls of her veins. Contaminated by my American ordinariness, condemned for my disloyalty, my veins are the equivalent of a genetic tourniquet. I am not a million percent Highland Scottish. I am not tribal. I have no patience with nostalgia. I've relinquished wonderful Old Africa and crossed the Atlantic to join the dull New World. And worst of all, I have Told All in an Awful Book, like on the *Jerry Springer Show*.

The man in Casper, Wyoming, whose job it was to interview candidates wishing to become naturalized American citizens in The Cowboy State had been in the military for most of his adult life. His jaw had been wired together and he was forced to speak between gritted teeth, which made him sound as if he were barely containing a deeply felt rage against the world in general and against future immigrants to the United States in particular. He asked me a few questions about the Constitution and the American War of Independence. He asked how many stars were on the American flag and what color they were. And then he got to the Deeply Personal Questions.

"Are you now or have you ever been a member of the Nazi Party?"

"No," I said.

"Are you now or have you ever been a member of the Communist Party?"

"No," I said.

"Do you," the man asked, "have a family history of insanity?"

In this situation, Mum would have felt the warm sensation of a student receiving an examination question on a subject for which she had prepared all her life. She would have settled herself comfortably in her chair, arranged herself for the long haul and begun with, "As a matter of fact, there is a long line of mental instability in our family going back centuries: funny moods, mental wobbliness, depression, that sort of thing."

But I, shaking my head for added emphasis, looked the man straight in the eye and answered firmly, "No."

Thus, having denied my own mother and most of her ancestors, I entered Scotland in the early autumn of 2002 as a foreigner. My brand-new blue American passport looked very flat and shiny, and as a consequence, a little counterfeit, as if I were a spy for hire, equipped with temporary documents. I rented a car and drove west across Scotland until the roads turned into single tracks and the scenery began to take over with craggy violence. Just like the postcards, there really were sheep everywhere and sheep had the right of way (they stood in the middle of the road and looked baleful as I crept around them), but once I got to Skye, the triangular yellow signs that warned of sheep on the road had been altered to depict elephants, camels and Cape buffalo. Beware elephants on the road. Beware camels on the road. Beware Cape buffalo on the road.

I leased a cottage for a week and then, of course, it rained. Not an ordinary sort of rain, or even an ordinarily heavy sort of rain, but the kind of rain that was like standing under the sea the moment Someone Almighty decided to tip it out on top of you. The wind blew so hard the car alarm kept going off. Seagulls gusted past the cottage windows, backward. For four days I stayed indoors, refusing to believe that weather like this could last forever. On the fifth day, I wrapped myself up from head to toe in waterproof materials and ventured out with map and notebook to a great chunk of wild land on the northwestern claw of the island.

I was guided as much by snatches of conversation I'd had with Mum and Granny over the years as I was by my map. The land, the sky and the sea were all the same rain shade of gray that made distinguishing landmarks impossible, but I eventually found the grand old house of Waternish Estate, a great crumbling building with black holes where its windows used to be, holes that made it look unseeing, un-alive. I parked along the roadside and walked onto the grounds, feeling like a trespasser not against whoever owned the place now but against Mum's riotously romantic idea of her ancestry.

Coming out into a clearing, I was struck immediately by the strange spectacle of a monkey puzzle tree growing on the edge of what had once been the lawn. I had seen old black-and-white photographs of this tree from the 1920s, but nothing could have prepared me for its utter South American foreignness on this wild, coastal Scottish property.

"Probably planted by Major Allan Macdonald in the early 1800s," Mum said. "The major took a great interest in horticulture and farming. He had a prize herd of Highland cattle and he also loved cairn terriers. He actually started the breed, or whatever you say when you invent a dog. He bred them to kill all the wild otters around the estate that were messing up his fishing."

Aside from the killing of otters (Mum had wept for a week after reading Gavin Maxwell's autobiography, *Ring of Bright Water*), it was clear that Major Allan Macdonald had Mum's firm stamp of approval. Being a loyal one million percent Scottish Highland Macdonald of Clanranald, Mum won't say a word against cairn terriers even though she bears a scar on her lip where one named Robert savaged her when she was a young woman. "Well, it was my fault," she said. "I surprised him and cairn terriers don't like surprises."

Major Allan's son, Captain Allan — known to the family as Muncle — was also fond of dogs and cattle. He sailed one of the last convict ships to Tasmania in the late 1840s. He took several cairn terriers with him on the journey, and family lore has it that he brought back two Tasmanian Palawa Aborigines in their place. Supposedly, the Aborigines lived, until their deaths, on Waternish Estate along with a pet deer that Muncle (an avid hunter) had blinded, but not killed, and a pack of yappy terriers.

I am haunted by those two alleged Palawa. God only knows what awful memories they stored inside their souls from their native land, but their ability to tell of their ordeals was locked in their tongues on this strange, Gaelic-speaking island. "By the 1820s horrible things were happening in Tasmania," Jan Morris writes in *Heaven's Command: An Imperial Progress*. "Sometimes the black people were hunted for fun . . . sometimes they were raped in passing, or abducted as mistresses or as slaves. The sealers of Bass Islands established a slave society of their own with harems of women, employing the well-tried discipline of slavery — clubbing, stringing up from trees, or flogging with kangaroo-gut whips. In one foray seventy aborigines were killed, the men shot, the women and children dragged from crevices in the rocks to have their brains dashed out."

On December 1, 1826, the Tasmanian *Colonial Times* announced, "We make no pompous display of Philanthropy. We say this unequivocally SELF DEFENCE IS THE FIRST LAW OF NATURE. THE GOVERNMENT MUST REMOVE THE NATIVES — IF NOT, THEY WILL BE HUNTED DOWN LIKE WILD BEASTS AND DESTROYED!"

At my most charitable, I imagine that

41

Muncle might have rescued the two Palawa, and brought them back to Waternish so that they might avoid the genocide that was surely their fate in Tasmania.

"I doubt it," Mum says. "I don't think Muncle was that sort of man."

I have seen photos of Muncle with his terriers and his deer, but the Palawa are ghosts, appearing nowhere. I have no way of knowing, even, what gender or age they were. So in the absence of any evidence I picture two homesick, middle-aged men sitting in this rain-lashed garden under a tree from South America with a blind deer, driven to distraction by ill-tempered and unpredictable terriers.

"That's so awful," I say to Mum. "Where are they buried?"

"Well, they wouldn't have been buried in the cemetery because they weren't Christians." Mum pauses. "They were heathens." I can tell from the way she says it that she likes that word — heathens — and its Somerset Maughamesque connotations. "But there's a very nice little pet cemetery behind the house. I suppose it's possible they're buried there."

"Buried with those snappy dogs," I say.

"Oh," Mum says, "I don't know. It wouldn't bother me." And then her eyes go a threatening yellow. "You're not going to put that in an Awful Book are you?" she says. "You'll have Aborigines crawling from one end of the island to the other, digging the place up looking for ancestors." Then she thinks about it. "Well, I suppose we don't own the estate anymore, so it doesn't matter."

Waternish Estate was sold to a Dutchman in the 1960s when Bad-tempered Donald died. In turn, the Dutchman sold a part of the estate to the Scottish singer-songwriter Donovan. Donovan was the first of the British musicians to adopt the flower-power image. He is most famous for the psychedelically fabulous smash hits "Sunshine Superman," "Season of the Witch" and "The Fat Angel," and for being the first high-profile British pop star to be arrested for the possession of marijuana. Donovan has a history of being deeply groovy and of being most often confused with Bob Dylan, which reportedly annoys Donovan quite a lot.

"Sometime in the early seventies, Bob Dylan bought part of the estate," Mum tells me. "But he put a water bed on the second floor of the house for whatever it is these hippies get up to, and it came crashing through the ceiling."

"Not Bob Dylan," I say. "Donovan."

"Who?" Mum says.

■ ■ ■ ■

The only land to which the Macdonalds of Waternish have any claim anymore are mounds in the graveyard of the ruined Trumpan Church near Waternish Estate. There are two small mounds with my grandparents in them and one larger mound containing a whole lot of my murderous, murdered ancestors. I drove toward the sea and found my grandparents' graves. I stared down at them, wondering which one was my grandfather and which my grandmother. Mum was still trying to remember the dates to put on her parents' headstones, and until then the graves were unmarked. "Isn't it dreadful," she says. "I just can't think when they were born." But this is how it has always been with our family. Whole lifetimes are reduced to one or two quixotic or iniquitous footnotes. When we were born and when we died are not important. After all, anyone can be born and die, but not everyone can Collect Aborigines or Begin a Breed of Dogs.

I turned and faced the Outer Hebrides. There, between me and the sea, was the mass grave of hundreds of my ancestors killed in one of the bloodiest episodes in Scottish history. So many died that a wall was pushed over the bodies in lieu of a proper burial and the battle became known as "The Spoiling of the Dyke." It's a story everyone in my family remembers, not because it was so brutal or because so many of our ancestors' lives were lost (that happened with depressing regularity if you were a Macdonald of Clanranald), but because it involved a rape, two fatal fires and a severed breast — a lively accumulation of drama, even by our standards.

Around 1577, a Macdonald defiled a Macleod maiden, "Or did something to annoy her at any rate," Mum says. In response — "a slight over-reaction in retrospect" — the MacLeods chased three hundred and ninety-five Macdonalds into St. Francis Cave on Eigg and lit a fire at the cave's entrance. The trapped Macdonalds suffocated. Clanranald, chief of the Macdonalds, spent all winter and most of the following spring plotting a suitable counter-revenge. "Yes, well," Mum says. "Highlanders aren't really turn-the-other-cheek sort of people." Accordingly, on the first Sunday in May 1578, Macdonald warriors, concealed by a thick fog, snuck up on Trumpan Church in which many of the MacLeods from nearby crofts had gathered for worship. The Macdonalds barred the church door and then set fire to the thatched roof. All the worshipping MacLeods were burned to death, except a young woman who managed to escape by squeezing through a narrow window, ripping off one of her breasts in the process.

I squint through the heavy rain and imagine that young woman, bleeding and in terror, running through the fog, across the heather to Dunvegan castle. Upon hearing her calls for help, the MacLeods seized their sacred banner — "The Fairy Flag," Mum says, enjoying this part of the story. "We're very mystical, very savage people you know" — and descended on the scorched remains of Trumpan Church, where they cornered and slaughtered the Macdonalds before they could flee. "Wonderfully tribal," Mum concludes approvingly.

I walked around to the small window of the ruined church. The window looked like something you might hope to shoot a skinny arrow through, but not anything you'd consider as a means of escape, even in dire circumstances. In any case, churches are supposed to be recognized as places you run into for refuge, not places you flee in terror. They are supposed to be universally recognized sanctuaries. But here my ancestors join all the worst villains in history — they are among those who have killed people in churches. I went back out to the view of the sea and kicked the spoiled dyke. A little black cloud scudded in from the Outer Hebrides and unloaded another small flood on me.

Cold and wet — waterproofing goes only so far when rain begins to rise up as well as fall down — I repaired to the nearest pub. Steaming in front of a large pint of bitter, surrounded by American tourists swapping ancestral anecdotes and swatches of tartan, I reflected that Mum would hate to live on the Isle of Skye now. The incessant battles over land, the blood feuds between clan and family — those are all over. The best she could hope for would be a bar brawl and even that — judging by the determinedly cheerful nature of the people in the pub — would be over before you could get yourself nicely settled into a ringside seat.

It is true that in Mum's opinion land is good, blood-soaked land is better and land soaked in the blood of one's ancestors is best. And by those criteria, the Isle of Skye is premium earth. But I am sure the American tourists would irritate her with their attempts to connect to a violence for which they no longer have any stomach. And the sheep would bore her silly. Because even painted up as camels, Cape buffalo and elephants, sheep are still just sheep.

NICOLA FULLER AND THE
FANCY DRESS PARTIES

*Mum and Auntie Glug as Alice and
the White Rabbit. Kenya, circa 1950.*

When she was six, Mum's parents went on
leave from Kenya to Britain, taking their
two children with them. Of that three-week
journey by ship from Mombasa to South-

49

ampton and back again, Mum remembers only three things: "They performed this ghastly ceremony when the ship crossed the equator. The passengers were dunked in buckets of water and beaten up with dead fish." Then Mum remembers the ship stopping at Gibraltar, where she was dragged by her parents to see the Barbary apes. "It was stinking hot and we had to haul up to see the Rock, which was plastered in ravens and these ferocious, scary monkeys." And finally Mum recalls, "The other thing — the most gruesome thing — was the Fancy Dress Party. It was awful, being paraded around the deck dressed up in some silly costume. I hated the whole ordeal."

"Then why did you participate, if it was so gruesome?"

"You had to," Mum says. "You were beaten into it."

"With dead fish?" I ask.

Mum gives me a look. "No. Not unless you also happened to be crossing the equator at that exact same moment."

So here we are: Mum, now in her early thirties, having apparently learned nothing from her experience as a child, dressing Vanessa and me up for the Davises' annual Fancy Dress, an event I might not have dreaded at all if Mum hadn't chosen costumes of such agonizing inventiveness that it's a wonder they didn't kill us.

"Why can't I be like Vanessa?" I asked.

"Because," Mum said.

"But I'm itchy," I complained.

Olivia was only four months old, too small to be anything murderous, so Mum had dressed her in a homemade, rainbow-colored, tie-dyed onesie as the Summer of Love. Vanessa was a Rose, hypoallergenic and splendid in a pink tutu, pink tights and pink ballet slippers. I was I Never Promised You a Rose Garden in an old vest and a pair of knickers inside an empty insecticide drum on which Mum had pasted a few pictures of weeds cut from the pages of *Farmers Weekly*.

"No one's going to understand what I am," I pointed out.

"The clever ones will," Mum said. "Now hold still. I don't want to poke your eyes out."

There was the sound of Mum attacking the insecticide drum with scissors.

"I think I'm getting a rash," I said. "I can feel bumps."

Mum started to sing, "I beg your pardon, I never promised you a rose garden. Along with the sunshine, there's gotta be a little rain sometime. . . ." There was a pause followed by a couple more violent assaults against the insecticide drum. Then Mum said to Vanessa, "Go to the kitchen and fetch me a knife, would you Vanessa? Ask July for a nice sharp one."

"I can't breathe," I said.

"Oh, buck up, Bobo."

"Wouldn't it be easier if I got out?"

"No, it wouldn't."

"But then you won't poke my eyes out."

"Whoever said anything about poking eyes out?"

"You did."

"Don't exaggerate."

I could hear Vanessa rustle demurely back into the room. "Thank you, *darling,*" Mum said. She only called one of us darling when she wanted to imply that the other was not, at that moment, darling. "You're such a big help," Mum said.

I didn't need to be on the outside of my insecticide drum to see the pink ruffles on Vanessa's tutu puffing up.

"Now hold still, Bobo."

There were flashes from a knife blade and two slits of light appeared.

"Are those near your eyes?"

"No," I said. And then I reconsidered my close escape. "Yes," I said. "Yes, very."

"There we go then," Mum said. "I'll just

get my Uzi and we'll be off."

I took a deep breath. "I don't want to go," I blurted with as much feeling as I could muster out of my nearly eight-year-old self. "I look stupid."

"Now look here," Mum said, "if you aren't careful, you'll get a jolly good hiding."

While Mum got her gun, I weighed up the cons of a jolly good hiding versus the cons of arriving at a Fancy Dress Party dressed in an insecticide drum. I decided, on balance, that at least there would be Sparletta Creme Soda and Willards Chips at the Fancy Dress Party and that at least the Davises didn't have frogs in their pool — or only a few. Not like our algae soup of a pool that had wild ducks, scorpions, thousands of frogs, tadpoles and the occasional Nile monitor. Plus, this would be my last party before I was packed off to boarding school forever and ever.

"Right," Mum said. I heard her check the Uzi magazine for rounds. We were a year into the worst part of the Rhodesian War, and ambushes and attacks against farmers had increased lately, especially where we lived on Robandi, right up against the Mozambique border where the view was spectacular but almost everything else was lousy.

In April 1966, the year before my parents

moved from Kenya to Rhodesia, the Zimbabwe African National Liberation Army (ZANLA) launched an attack against government forces to protest Ian Smith's Unilateral Declaration of Independence from Britain. The uprising was swiftly and definitively suppressed. Seven ZANLA troops lost their lives. No Rhodesian forces died. After that, the war simmered along mildly with the odd attack or ambush here and there until 1974, when the ten-year conflict in neighboring Mozambique between the Marxist Front for the Liberation of Mozambique rebels (FRELIMO) and the colonial Portuguese ended, and a new confrontation between the FRELIMO government and Rhodesian and South African–backed Mozambican National Resistance forces (RENAMO) began. Then, as if the uptick in violence in the neighboring state were contagious, the war in Rhodesia also picked up momentum. ZANLA forces based in Mozambique under the guerilla-friendly FRELIMO government came over the border into Rhodesia to lay land mines and conduct raids. War became our climate, something you didn't feel you could do much about and that you might remark on casually, using the same language you might use to describe the weather: "Phew, things are getting hot this week."

We accepted the war as one of the prices that had to be paid for Our Freedom, although it was a funny sort of Freedom that didn't include being able to say what you wanted about the Rhodesian government or being able to write books that were critical of it. And for the majority of the country, Freedom did not include access to the sidewalks, the best schools and hospitals, decent farming land or the right to vote. It now seems completely clear to me, looking back, that when a government talks about "fighting for Freedom" almost every Freedom you can imagine disappears for ordinary people and expands limitlessly for a handful of people in power.

"Bullets, lipstick, sunglasses. Off we go. Come on, Bobo, quick march."

My feet poked out of two holes in the drum's lid. I couldn't walk very well. I had to waddle like a penguin. This amused Vanessa, and her peals of laughter echoed around inside the insecticide drum. Mum, with Olivia on her hip, helped me out of the big door, down the rough stone steps and onto the veranda. "Don't fall," Vanessa said, barely able to contain the hope in her voice. It was very hot inside the drum and sweat poured into my already stinging eyes and onto my increasingly stinging rash.

"I'm boiling," I whined.

"One more word out of you," Mum warned.

We scuffled across the yard and into the driveway, and arrived at Lucy, the mine-proofed Land Rover, where a problem presented itself. I didn't fit through any of the doors.

"Oh dear," Mum said. "An unforeseen hitch." There was a silence while she had a think. I pictured her biting the inside of her lower lip and frowning. When she spoke again, she sounded struck by inspiration. "We'll put her in the back." She paused. "Darling," she said, not to me, "go and fetch July and Violet."

So Vanessa called July from the kitchen and she fetched Violet from the laundry. Then there was general hilarity while July and Violet each considered how amazing it was that the madam had put her young daughter into an insecticide drum. Mum explained that when she was in labor with me in England, the radio was playing "I Never Promised You a Rose Garden," which was prophetic because when I arrived, I really was, as promised, Not a Rose Garden (Mum has refused to waver from this story, even though I have since discovered this song became a hit for Lynn Anderson a full year and a half *after* I was born and therefore could not have been playing when she was in labor with me).

"She had yellow skin and black hair. That's why we call her Bobo," Mum explained, "because she looked just like a little baboon."

Violet and Vanessa dissolved into more conspiratorial giggling.

"See?" Mum said, "Violet thinks your costume's amusing."

"Could we just get on with this?" I said.

So July and Violet each seized an ankle and thrust me into the vehicle while I stood rigid inside my insecticide drum. I could smell the greasy-meat scent of the dogs' supper on July's clothes and the green laundry soap on Violet's hands and arms, but now the usually comforting domestic scents had an isolating, excluding effect. The dogs circled around us and whacked the drum with their tails. Their excited panting made me feel even hotter.

"Right," Mum said. "Off we go." She climbed into the Land Rover and Vanessa-darling got in on the passenger side. "Hold on to the baby," Mum said, handing Olivia to Vanessa. Then she whistled and a couple of lapfuls of dogs leaped in with them. The Land Rover jerked off down the hill and bumped past the orchard. I could feel it go

57

over the culvert at the bottom of the driveway where the cobra lived. I yawed against the window as Mum took a left onto the main road at the bottom of the farm. I pictured Vanessa, billowing pinkly in the front seat, the wind flapping her two long, blond braids in which Mum had entwined pink and white roses made out of loo paper. And I pictured Mum driving, dogs on her lap, her gun out the window, checking her hair and lipstick in the rearview mirror.

"I can't stand up back here!" I cried, "slow down!" But my protests were lost under the roar and rattle of Lucy's engine. The fact that I wasn't, at that moment, being beaten by dead fish was small comfort.

Thirty years, two countries and four farms later, Vanessa, Mum and I were sitting under the Tree of Forgetfulness at Mum and Dad's fish and banana farm on the Middle Zambezi River. Something about the quality of heat, and the itchy burn from the windborne, stinging hairs of buffalo bean, reminded me of the day of that long ago Fancy Dress Party.

"Do you remember when you made me be I Never Promised You a Rose Garden at the Davises' Annual Christmas Fancy Dress party?" I asked Mum.

"Oh God," Mum said. "Here we go. Another traumatizing repressed memory come back to haunt us." She looked around. Then she flung her arms in the air. "Shrink! Someone fetch the child a shrink!" Mum does exactly this gesture when her drink runs dry at a party: she flings her arms in the air and shrieks, "Drought! Nicola Fuller of Central Africa is experiencing severe drought!"

"Olivia was the Summer of Love and Vanessa was a Rose, all dressed up in a pink tutu," I said.

"Was I?" Vanessa said.

"Yes," I said.

"No, I wasn't," Vanessa said. "I was From Russia with Love."

I frowned. "Really?"

"Yes," Vanessa said firmly, "in a hat made out of fermenting, flea-infested carpet. And I had to wear a baking red shirt, billowing black pants and Mum's riding boots."

"I think you're mixing up fancy dress parties. I distinctly remember you were a rose," I said.

"I wish," Vanessa said.

"From Russia with love I fly to you," Mum sang. She paused and went on conversationally, "I remember that film. I made Dad drive all the way to Nairobi so we could watch it. They had vodka shots lined up at the bar." She sniffed. "Hm, well, the film must have made quite an impression on me if I wasted a perfectly good carpet on Vanessa's fancy dress costume." She took a breath and continued to sing, "Much wiser since my good-bye to you . . ."

"See?" Vanessa said.

"I've traveled the world," Mum sang, "to learn I must return to Russia with loooooooooo-oooove!"

"Well, I remember I had to sit in the back of the Land Rover and you, Mum, Olivia and the dogs sat in the front," I said.

"Straitjacket!" Mum shouted.

"And only the front part of the Land Rover was mine proofed," I said.

"Tranquilizers!" Mum shrieked.

"So if we'd gone over a land mine, you, Olivia, Mum and the dogs would have been fine. But I would have been blown up. Wouldn't I, Mum?"

Vanessa started laughing. "That's hilarious," she said.

"Wouldn't I have been blown up if you'd gone over a mine, Mum?" I asked.

Mum let her arms drop by her side. "I suppose that's right," she said. She paused, and then continued, "But if I'd known then that you were going to grow up and write that Awful Book, I might have actually aimed for one."

"Mum!"

Mum sighed. "You know, you're just like Christopher bloody Robin. That wretched child also grew up and wrote an Awful Book even after all those lovely stories and poems his father wrote for him. He went on and on about what a rotten parent A. A. Milne had been and about how A. A. Milne hadn't hugged Christopher bloody Robin enough." Mum, a dedicated fan of all things Pooh, shuddered. "Luckily," she said, "I don't think many people read it and I am sure hardly anyone took it very seriously."

Our family's overwhelming attachment to animals and their apparent lukewarm attachment to their own offspring (quite different from a passionate connection to "blood") go back at least as far as my grandmother's childhood, which is where anything close to reliable oral history ends. Mum's younger sister, Auntie Glug, remembers my grandmother as a remarkably efficient caretaker and a very capable nurse, deeply interested in her children's welfare but quite unable to hug her children.

"Yuck," said Mum, whose own maternal hugs are stiff, reluctant and brief. "We just weren't raised that way." And then her eyes went pale and she spoke to me very slowly,

Mum with her first best friend, Stephen Foster. Kenya, circa 1946.

as if explaining her culture to an alien visitor. "We are terribly British: stiff upper lip, no public displays of affection. It's how my mother was raised, and it's how we were raised — and I don't think it did any of us any harm."

I refrained from pointing out that my grandmother, Mum and Auntie Glug had all spent time in institutions for the mentally unhinged. In any case, Mum would have countered the diagnosis, "Highly strung, I think you mean. There's nothing wrong with being that kind of bonkers. It has nothing to do with not being hugged enough and everything to do with being so well bred, and that leads to chemical imbalance. We're like difficult horses or snappy dogs; it's not our fault. It's in the blood."

In keeping with their arm's-length style of parenting, the Macdonalds of Waternish were remarkably unimaginative when it came to naming their children. Boys were Allan or Donald and, at a stretch, Patrick. Girls were Flora. My grandmother, an unwelcome surprise, arriving twelve years later than her siblings, was Edith, but everyone called her Donnie. Before Donnie reached her teens, her father, Allan Macdonald, died. How he died is a matter of some dispute. Mum says Allan Macdonald broke his neck in a riding accident, but a distant Macdonald relative told me that he died from a bad cold.

"Well, that might be," Mum says impatiently, "but a broken neck certainly didn't help."

In any case, the result was the same. Granny's father was dead and her bad-tempered brother Donald inherited the estate. The death duties were crippling. Bad-tempered Donald sold every valuable painting and antique on the estate. He divorced his wife, citing exasperation at the way she ate apples, and he sent his son, Mad Cousin Patrick, away with her. Then he retreated to a tower on the north side of the house where he stayed for the remainder of his life while dry rot ravaged the rooms and a thick growth of green slime crawled over the cold stone walls down the hallways and into the kitchens.

Meanwhile, Granny's mother, who had not been provided for in her husband's will because everyone kept thinking she'd die in the night of a bladder infection, sat in a basket chair in her bedroom waiting in vain for the Grim Reaper. It was so cold in the house that she went everywhere with an Aladdin paraffin lamp and she always wore at least five cardigans, the longest one on the bottom, layers and layers of shorter ones on top of that and a thick shawl around her shoulders.

And then there was my grandmother's elder brother, Shell-shocked Allan, a desperately good-looking but very sensitive man who had run away at the age of seventeen to fight in the First World War and had been gassed in the trenches, leaving him delicate and scarred. He kept a hundred cats and carried on a secret marriage with the village postmistress, with whom he had one son, named, of course, Allan (but known as Wee Allan to distinguish him from his father, which worked well until Wee Allan grew into a six-foot-four man of considerable if gentle bulk).

"So Waternish House was quite suffocating by then, full to overflowing with damaged people and Muncle's stuffed animals," Mum says. "Moldy heads with bared yellow teeth and glassy eyes all leering down from the walls."

My grandmother escaped this Dickensian shelter to stay with the crofters who lived and worked on the estate. From them she picked up fluent Gaelic. She learned how to sneak up on razor fish by walking backward along the beach. She collected carrageen and swam in the warm currents of the Atlantic with wild otters and seals. She galloped her family's crossbred Arabian Highland horses bareback across the heather. She spent her nights in the natural, warm clatter of the housekeeper's lodge, a cottage made entirely of corrugated iron, so that nobody could hear anybody speak whenever the wind blew or whenever it rained, which was almost all the time, so no one bothered much with conversation. It was, in many ways, a charmed and feral childhood.

Still, it was no wonder that when friends offered my grandmother free berth to Kenya in exchange for acting as au pair to their children, she fled the island of her ancestors and headed for the colonies. She was twenty years old. Until the day she left for Africa, she'd never been more than a hundred miles from her home. On her journey she took the native intelligence of her crofter upbringing; a suitcase of sensible clothes; a diary in which she recorded the day's temperature and any other notable occurrence; and several dense biographies of various members of the British royal household, past and present.

Fairly soon after reaching Kenya, Donnie met and married Roger "Hodge" Huntingford. For eleven years Donnie and Hodge tried to have a child, but the massive quantities of quinine my grandmother took to prevent and treat malaria also acted as an abortive. Not until the Second World War, when my grandfather was stationed in Burma and my grandmother had gone back to live on Waternish Estate, did she manage to carry a child to term.

Once the war was over, my grandparents returned to Kenya with two-year-old Nicola in tow. "The men went out first to set things up again," Mum says. "And then my mother and I came out on the first ship to bring women and children — a converted troop carrier, the RMS *Alcantara*." Mum pauses. "In my memory, there were ten thousand women and children on that ship and one man — Mr. Branson, the haberdasher from

Eldoret — but that can't be right. Can it? Maybe there were two thousand women and children, and Mr. Branson the haberdasher."

On the train from Mombasa to Eldoret, Mum ran up and down the dining car and ate all the butter off the tables — pounds and pounds of butter, rationed in Britain but here for the taking — and by the time she got to Eldoret, she had acidosis. "I was seriously, seriously sick and had to be whipped straight off to Doctor Reynolds for a liver remedy." Mum blinks at me in surprise. "Where were all the grown-ups while I was busy wolfing down the butter? I nearly killed myself with greed and no one stopped me."

Eldoret is a town south of the Cherangani Hills on the Uasin Gishu plateau, close to Kenya's border with Uganda. Originally known as 64, it was sixty-four miles from the head of the newly built Uganda Railway, but then the settlement became more established and the settlers cast around for something that sounded more romantic — less like the location of a prison camp — and someone came up with Eldoret, taken from the Masai word *eldare* meaning "stony river."

"It was a bit bleak and windy sometimes and it could be very cold up at six thousand feet," Mum says. "We had to light a fire almost every night. But compared to gloomy old Britain after the war, it was ecstasy. For one thing, the quality of light so close to the equator! And for another thing, the space. You could look across the plateau all the way to the horizon and you would see uninterrupted land for as far as anyone could hope to walk in a single day."

My grandfather worked as a government agricultural extension officer, going off on safari for two or three weeks at a time to remote parts of the country and leaving my grandmother and Mum "up country." To begin with, until they could find a proper house, the Huntingfords lived in a tiny rented bungalow on the grounds of the Kaptagat Arms, the estate of Zoe Foster, whose husband had been a white hunter in Uganda.

"The husband was gone by the time we showed up. I think he had been eaten by a lion or gored by a buffalo or whatever happened to those white-hunter types," Mum says. "Anyway, Zoe seemed perfectly happy. She had two sons, a beautiful blond daughter called Mary and lots of animals. There was always a vicious but effective mongoose resident in the house, excellent for killing snakes — just like Rikki-Tikki-Tavi. Oh, and her garden was the most exciting in the whole area — a stream, a maze, beds of rhododendrons and roses, lavender and peonies, and a vivid lawn strewn with hippo and elephant skulls that the husband had shot over the years." Mum's voice takes on a singsong quality, as if she is reading from a storybook: "It was fantastic. I used to run away from our bungalow, which was on the edge of the estate, and go over to the main house and play in her garden with my first best friend, Stephen Foster." Mum smiles at the memory. "Stephen and I used to take turns pushing each other on his tricycle. We wore matching romper suits. We had tea parties. We went everywhere together, hand in hand."

"Stephen was one of Zoe's sons?" I guess.

Mum frowns. "No, no, no," she says. "Stephen wasn't her son. Stephen was her chimpanzee."

There is a small, appalled pause while I try — and fail — to imagine sending one of my toddlers off to play with a chimpanzee (quite apart from the Jane Goodall abuse-of-the-animal concerns).

"Weren't your parents worried he would bite you?" I ask.

Mum gives me a look as if I have just called Winnie-the-Pooh a pedophile, "Stephen? Bite me? Not at all, we were best friends. He was a very, very nice, very civilized chimpanzee. Anyway, my mother didn't worry about me too much. She knew I would always be all right because everywhere I went Topper came with me."

"And Topper was?"

"A dog my father had rescued," Mum says.

Which might explain why, when I was packed off to boarding school in Rhodesia for three months at a time, and missed the lousy farm with every fiber of my being, my own rescued dog wrote me letters more regularly than Mum did, and certainly with more affection:

"My Dearest Bobo," Jason King (my dachshund, bailed out of the Umtali, Rhodesia, chapter of the Society for the Prevention of Cruelty to Animals), wrote in January 1977:

I've been out riding with Mum and the horses every day this week. I've learned how to climb trees to chase lizards. I keep getting stuck high up in the Flamboyants and July has to climb up and rescue me.

Sally has been very naughty and went hunting for three nights last week. She took Bubbles with her. I think they were chasing baboons. Sally came home with a bleeding tongue and sore paws and dripping with ticks. It serves her right. Bubbles got all the way to the river before one of the boys saw him. They were both lucky not to get caught in a snare.

I hope you are working hard at your lessons and being good for your matrons and teachers. Tell Vanessa that she is supposed to share her tuck with you. I miss you very, very much, especially at tea time. I sleep on your bed every night and on your chair all day.

Lots and lots of love,

Your beloved friend and the biggest supporter of the Bobo Fuller Fan Club,

Jason King

oxo

ROGER HUNTINGFORD'S WAR

Hodge with Nandi tribesmen in Kenya, circa 1930.

Auntie Glug, Mum's younger sister, now lives in a small village in Scotland with her husband, Sandy; a passionately adored dog called India and a couple of cats. Their three children are grown and have left home, but Langlands Lodge feels like a place that has never given up on raising children. Its prevailing odors remain nursery comforting: warm toast, freshly brewed tea and stewed plums. If my parents had been killed in the Rhodesian War, Vanessa, Olivia and I would have come to live in Langlands with Auntie Glug and Uncle Sandy. In this way, the house has always felt like a refuge, a place of certainty and safety. I sleep profoundly here (fourteen hours at a stretch) and I eat without restraint, grazing my way steadily through Uncle Sandy's casseroles, his wheatie buns, his greenhouse grapes (a habit that has earned me the Langlands' nickname Niece-Weevil).

Auntie Glug hasn't lived in Africa since 1967, but she still dresses like a Kenyan settler woman of a certain era — men's clothes, work boots, a red handkerchief tucked into her sleeve — and she smokes like a soldier. The boxes of photos and letters that I dig out from under the stairs smell of her cigarettes but also of my grandfather's pipe tobacco, the homegrown, home-cured crop he used to hang in his garage in England. The smell of rum and earth are as fresh for me as the instant memory this scent retrieves of his guffawing, irreverent laugh.

Auntie Glug has inherited from her parents a holy belief in the restorative nature of gardening and animals and she is unapologetically earthy. Several years ago she went to India and came back wearing salwar kameez and eating with her fingers (the salwar kameez didn't last — not practical in the winter and she kept setting them alight with her cigarettes). She is also the only person I have ever met who has returned from that country enthusiastically endorsing its latrines. "Very sensible," she said, "all that healthy squatting."

From where I am sitting in her morning room, she appears in her garden as something ancient and essential in our people. Warped by the old Victorian glass windows; morphed by an old shirt of my grandfather's and a pair of tie-waisted corduroys; shadowed by India, over whom she bends once in a while to consult and pet, she gives the impression of being ageless, genderless, doggedly Macdonald of Clanranald but also a product of East Africa, of that particular time and place when there were really no limits on how well or badly, sanely or madly a white person had to behave. "Don't talk to me about behaving," Auntie Glug says, giving one of her badger growls. "Bugger that." (As a result of Auntie's standard non-

74

conformity — gardening until midnight while teaching herself Spanish, controlling air traffic over Dundee while knitting *and* teaching herself Spanish — it is sometimes a little difficult to tell when her natural eccentricity crosses into territory better understood by the professionals.)

No Macdonald of Clanranald is entirely at home in a house that does not have animals *and* ghosts. Accordingly, there is in Langlands Lodge the ghost of a little white dog (killing, as it were, two birds with one stone). My cousins say they've heard it clatter up and down the stairs at night, and until my grandmother died in 1993, she saw it with such persistence she began to doubt it was a ghost at all and began to leave milk and food for it on the landing.

Uncle Sandy is two million percent Scottish and a pilot. He plays the bagpipes at all our family funerals and weddings, kitted out in the proper attire (a mere glimpse of his bagpipes and sporran makes Mum weep). Uncle Sandy can tell you next week's weather just by looking at the clouds over the Sidlaw Hills; he can dead reckon the speed of the wind to within a knot or two and he can tell, without looking, when the rooks have come in from the fields to roost in the forest near Langlands. Because of his job, he is off traveling much of the time, but when he is home, he stations himself in the kitchen and cooks the kitchen to a steam, as if the act of leaving behind frozen tubs of chili and freshly baked bread and bottles of plum jam means that he is never really gone from Langlands.

It is in this creaking, ghosted home, fragrant with Uncle Sandy's cooking, the BBC ancient-rhyming the *Shipping Forecast* from the kitchen and the old grandfather clock in the dining room creaking as if time hurt to tell, that I touch the corner of my grandfather's war in two scraps of paper. The first is his enlisting agreement, signed June 13, 1940. "I swear by Almighty God that I will be faithful and bear true allegiance to His Majesty King George the Sixth, His Heirs and Successors, and that I will as in duty bound, honestly and faithfully defend His Majesty, His Heirs and Successors, in Person, Crown and Dignity against all enemies, and will observe and obey all orders of His Majesty, His Heirs and Successors, and of the General and Officers set over me. So help me God."

There appears my grandfather's signature.

Below that was written "Have you received a notice paper stating the liabilities you are incurring by enlisting?" Next to which my grandfather had penned, "Yes."

"And do you understand and are you willing to accept them?"

"Yes."

My grandfather's father was a vicar in the Church of England. "There are bishops and vicars going back as far as you like on that side of the family," Mum says. "Scholars, you understand. It wasn't as if God sent down a great bolt of lightning and inspired them — nothing that easy — not like preachers and missionaries. All of our family had to go to something like university for seven years — ages and ages, in any case — and speak Latin and Greek and Hebrew. One of the Huntingford bishops is buried under the floor of Winchester Cathedral, or there's a plaque there, anyway, commemorating him. He was head of the college. No one liked him very much. I think his flock — or whatever it is that Bishops have — mutinied."

At the turn of the century, my grandfather's father looked at his growing family — three young boys — and decided that he couldn't raise them on a vicar's income in England. So like a lot of other people buying into the myth of East Africa's munificence, he thought he'd try to make a go of it in Kenya. "Everyone thought they could go out

77

there and grow coffee, but it wasn't as easy as it sounded and my grandfather wasn't the least bit interested in coffee, he was too spiritual, too other-worldly, too learned and scholarly to come to grips with farming, so that failed," Mum says. "He built a church somewhere, but the thing burned down. And then the youngest of the three boys, Tony, became terribly ill."

The child was raced to the Eldoret hospital, but he died of septicemia. He was ten years old. "I don't think the family ever recovered from Tony's death. His parents went into a deeply profound mourning. They didn't really care about money or much of anything practical to begin with, but after Tony died, they gave up caring about worldly things altogether."

My grandfather's oldest brother, Uncle Dicken, grew up to become a linguist and an anthropologist, and he wrote the first dictionary of the Nandi people. "He lived with the Nandi for ten years, knew all their customs and everything. This was back in the late 1920s and 30s when it wasn't very fashionable to go off and live with the natives, but he didn't do it in a creepy sort of way, he was *studying* the people." Mum narrows her eyes at me and says, "I just know you're going to put that in an Awful

Book and make it sound as if he went native, but he didn't. He was very British and very proper, and I am sure he didn't touch a young Nandi maiden or anything horrible like that."

This remark made me think Uncle Dicken must have done something to unnerve Mum, an impression that was enhanced when I discovered a paper titled "Sexual Growth Among the Nandi of Kenya" that cited his work. The sex life of a Nandi boy, according to the research of my great-uncle Dicken, "begins as soon as he has emerged from the seclusion of circumcision (kakoman tum) and a girl's when she reaches the age of puberty, i.e. about twelve. . . ."

My grandfather, Roger "Hodge," taught himself engineering and was hired to build the branch railway line from Eldoret to Kitale. "He had a donkey for transport," Mum says, "but the donkey fell in love with a herd of zebra and ran away to be with them. After that Dad had to use a bicycle."

It wasn't long after losing his donkey and taking up with a bicycle that my grandfather met and married my grandmother. Then war broke out and everyone reassessed their idea of home and loyalty, and my grandparents found themselves back in Skye from where my grandfather enlisted, lying that his mother was "Scotch" so that he could join up with the Cameron Highlanders. Seeing that he had grown up and worked in Kenya, the war board sent him to Burma and put him in charge of Nigerian troops.

"Well, you know how the Brits are," my grandfather told me once when my grandparents came out to visit us in Malawi. "They don't know there is a bloody great difference between a Nigerian and a Kenyan, let alone between a Kikuyu and a Kalenjin or an Igbo and a Hausa." My grandfather chewed on the end of his pipe, and belched a cloud of fragrant tobacco at me. "Can't say I thought much of Nigeria," he said. "All the Brits thought it was the prime spot, but it was swampy hot, for one thing, and smothered in mosquitoes for another. Burma wasn't too bad. At least there was the war to take your mind off the bloody humidity."

My grandfather had amused gray eyes and a magnificently unapologetic Roman nose. Throughout the time I knew him, he talked about Burma now and again, but in disconnected snatches, as if his memories were like the bouts of amebic dysentery that occasionally haunted him after the war — appearing without warning, sometimes violently, and then disappearing just as suddenly.

At some point during the war, my grandfather was wounded. "In Burma, I think. I don't know how," Mum says. "Of course, we didn't really talk about it. I suppose shrapnel or something. He had this tennis ball–sized lump on his hip. Glug and I always begged him, 'Show us your war wound! Show us your war wound!' and he would drop his shorts so we could admire it. And then the next thing was, 'Daddy, take your teeth out!' because everyone had false teeth in those days. As soon as they turned forty, that was it — off they all went to the dentist — out with the old and in with the snappers."

But Auntie Glug says, "No, no, no. It wasn't shrapnel in Burma. It was a rock in Nigeria. I'm sure of it. Someone threw a rock at him and he ended up with a very impressive lump on his hip." She waves her cigarette at me. "I'm convinced that's how he got his wound." And she seems so certain that I consider accepting her version of events until my cousin Cait and I discover a telegram in the bottom drawer of the Welsh dresser in the Langlands dining room:

Priority Mrs. EMB Huntingford
c/o Mrs Macdonald
Waternish House
Isle of Skye

Report received from India that Lieutenant R.L. Huntingford Queens Own Cameron Highlanders posted Black Watch serving with Nigeria Regiment was wounded in Burma on 7ᵗʰ March 1945. The Army Council express sympathy. Letter follows shortly.
Under Secretary for State for War.

Underneath the telegram my grandfather has written, "Correct report should have read 'wounded but remains on duty.' The R.A.F. dropped a 500 Ib bomb on the road in the middle of 5NR instead of on the JAPS!!!"

Cait and I turn the paper over, but that is all that has been written. The telegram leaves the cause of the lump on my grandfather's hip almost as confused as it was before. In the end, it seems safest to say that my grandfather was wounded at least once and possibly twice during the war, but whether it was a rock in Nigeria or the five hundred pounds of friendly fire in Burma that gave him the lump, we'll never know.

In 1943, my grandfather was posted briefly on the west coast of Scotland to guard against German warships in the Minch. His batman was from Inverness and so for a few glorious months from the late summer to the early winter of 1943, the war became a family affair — the batman able to visit his people in Inverness and my grandfather able to spend time at Waternish. The crofters on the Isle of Skye took to calling my grandfather "Major Macdonald," perhaps because he bore such a striking resemblance to my grandmother's gentle, shell-shocked brother Allan. "I think it must have been a happy time for my parents," Mum says. By which she means she was conceived.

In late 1943, my grandfather returned to Burma, and my grandmother — finally able to hold on to a pregnancy in the malaria-free chill of a British winter — went to the south of England for her war effort. She worked as a farm laborer near Southampton and boarded with a rich widow in a grand old house nearby. The widow, Catherine Angleton, had a wooden leg as a result of a bout with cancer, "but she dressed very nicely with stockings, tweed skirts and very good shoes," Mum says, "so you really couldn't tell."

As a major port and industrial area, Southampton had been a particular target of the Luftwaffe during the war. At the end of February 1944, when my grandmother was four and a half months pregnant, there was a major raid on the city. "Apparently, every time there was a bomb I jumped," Mum tells me. "I'm very sensitive to loud noises. It's why I always look a bit sour at children's birthday parties in case someone pops a balloon." Recognizing that air raids didn't suit the temperament of her fetus and fearing there would be more attacks on the town, my grandmother took the train up to Waternish to wait out the pregnancy.

Telegrams jolted from Skye to Burma to inform my grandfather about the birth of his daughter. "I saw a letter he wrote to his mother from Burma saying that he was very excited about having a little girl," Mum says. "But of course he didn't see me until I was over a year old, and when he did finally see me, he picked me up and promptly dropped me on my head." Mum preempts my wisecrack, "Yes, well a lot of things have been blamed on that little incident."

But the clearest thing I learned about my grandfather's war — and about his character — was from an undated letter written to him by one of his Nigerian troops whose obviously warm relationship with my grandfather seemed to exceed the startling, colonial-era salutation that begins:

Dear Master
    Will you tell me your present condition?

And what news of your family? I hope everyone is 50/50. As for myself, I want to report to you of this: we are no longer at Sandoway but in a township twenty-five miles to Rangoon. We left Sandoway on the 23rd of December 1945 to come here. From what I can see, Rangoon is a very big place but I can't inform you that it is a nice place. Above all, it is a stinking hole, smelly and filthy.

John Okongo, right. Burma, circa 1943.

Our current work is boring. We have about 4,000 Japs prisoners staying here with us and our only task is to guard them. That is all the work of 5 Nigeria Battalion. It is not hard work. But upon all that, everywhere else is off limits to us and the worst is there is no prospect of our going home.

So beloved master, that is all the news from the township. I hope you are doing well. Oh! I hope you will be kind enough to see about the picture I asked to send me.

I beg to pen down.

Thanks.

Yours,

John Okongo

Nicola Huntingford Learns to Ride

Circa 1947–1950

Mum and Nane. Kenya, circa 1954.

If she had known then the score and depth of the tragedy that was to come, Mum might have borne the insults of her childhood with more fortitude, but the pathos and the gift of life is that we cannot know which will be our defining heartbreak, or our most victorious joy. And so for a few years from around the time Mum turned three, an accumulation of what she considered truly dreadful events occurred. And because they were the first real insults of her so-far small life, they remain vivid and searing for her even now.

First, her sister, Glennis (Auntie Glug), was born — she had yellow curls, dimples on each cheek and a willful, devious nature. "She managed to have some sort of seizure when she was quite young," Mum says. "After that, my parents were terrified of smacking her in case she got herself into a state and had another fit. So no matter which of us had been naughty, I always got whacked and Glug got away with smirking at me."

Then my grandparents left the paradise of the bungalow at the Kaptagat Arms and rented an old army officers' mess closer to the town of Eldoret. My grandfather knocked rooms around to create a home out of the barracks. "It was very long and narrow," Mum says, "but my father was very clever with stonework and building. He made false beams in the sitting room to make it look ye olde, and built a wonderful stone fireplace."

There was no indoor plumbing so hot water was carried into the tub from the kitchen. The choo was a decent trek down to the bottom of the garden, "and often filled with bees and sometimes snakes," Mum says, "which terrified me and contributed to a lifetime of reluctant bowels." After dark, each family member was given a chamber pot, "gently steaming away under the bed and rusting the bed springs," Mum says. "At bedtime, Glug and I had to sit on our pots until we performed. Ages and ages sometimes we had to sit there. Out of sheer boredom we used to have races sitting on our pots, hopping them across the bedroom floor."

Glug was always getting malaria because she would threaten to have a fit every time anyone tried to make her take a pill. "Doctor Reynolds had to drive out from Eldoret to give her injections," Mum says. "Glennis would flip herself backward and forward across the room to get away from him and he'd have to try to catch her. One time he made a dive for her and he got his foot stuck in her chamber pot. I remember him skipping around the room in fury. Of course we were both wheezing with laughter, malaria injection quite forgotten."

Baths were taken under the vicious supervision of a drunken ayah, Cherito, who smacked Mum forcefully and repetitively but without any evident cause, as if she were merely practicing shot put or tennis and Mum's body was in the way of a particularly powerful swing (Glug, however, escaped the unpredictable violence of even Cherito's drunken temper, so ingrained was the Legend of Her Seizures and the fear that she'd have another one at the slightest provocation). "My parents would be in the sitting room or on the veranda, quite happily relaxing with some of my mother's homemade wine while Cherito was swatting me around the bathroom, so they knew nothing of what was happening. And Glug never uttered a peep about it because it was all very good entertainment for her."

My grandmother made wine out of potatoes, raisins, barley, figs — whatever she could get her hands on. "It was delicious, but she had no control over how strong each batch would be," Mum says. "It was well known for visitors to leave our house and get terribly confused and end up in the wrong district — and sometimes the wrong country. They'd be on their way to Kitale and end up in Bungoma. Or they'd be expected in Kapsabet but find themselves in Uganda."

With only the bitterly resented Glug for

company, Mum missed Stephen Foster terribly. The donkey, Suk, which my grandmother had bought as a replacement best friend was a big disappointment. In my mother's telling, he had a willful and devious nature, much like Glug, except with ears and a tail and without the Perfected Art of the Seizure. "Suk was not at all your storybook donkey," Mum says. "To get anywhere at all, I had to be dragged around by a syce. The donkey sneered at him, ignored me and brayed like a steam engine. I think it was humiliating for all of us."

And finally, most awful of all, it was decided that it was time for Mum to attend the convent, a school run by Irish nuns about half a mile away from their new home. Every morning, she was put into her uniform, a blue skirt and white shirt with a wide-brimmed black hat, "To keep the African sun off our faces." She was loaded onto the sulking Suk and hauled to school by the syce. Then the syce and Suk would wait under the eucalyptus trees for three hours until Mum's classes were over. After that, she would be put on the donkey, the donkey would be untied and the syce would be dragged from the end of the halter rope as Suk fled for the comforts of home.

As she got older, Mum was allowed to

ride Suk over to the school alone. "By then my legs were long enough, and I could just about kick the wretched beast into action." She tied the donkey up under the eucalyptus tree and went in to lessons. "Nicola is a disruptive influence in the class," her school report read. Mum found learning difficult. She showed early promise as an artist, but the nuns didn't care about art. Numbers made no sense to her at all, and even words were hard for her to grasp, "Our parents read to us every night, Rudyard Kipling, Ernest Thompson Seton, that kind of thing. I adored stories and books, but I struggled with the nuns and their dreary lessons and it took me ages to learn how to read."

Instead, she entertained herself by trying to coax one of the many cats that hunted in the school drains to come and sit on her lap. If the cat couldn't be persuaded into the classroom, Mum jumped out of the window after it. And then, since she was not Catholic — "Anglican, of course!" — and therefore could not be made to kneel in the chapel with the other recalcitrant girls fingering their way through endless rosaries, she would be banished to sit under the eucalyptus trees, which she found agreeable enough. She spent her time drawing in the dirt, peeling the bark off the trees, lolling on Suk's back, staring up into the leaves pulsing against the sun-stained sky and daydreaming until she calculated it was time to go home. Then she untethered the donkey, grasped her arms around his neck and galloped back for tea.

Mum has to go back sixty years to recall the convent and those nuns, but the bits she pulls up from her memory are bright and sharp, kept polished and immediate by a deep and abiding hatred for the place and for the women who ran it. "Sister Bede used to smack our hands with a ruler so hard the ruler often broke. Sister Philip caned us around the back of the legs until she raised welts." Mum pauses and her eyes go pale. "They smacked me and punished me and banished me, but it just made me more difficult and defiant and determined not to learn."

One day the nuns blocked all the drains and gassed the school's stray cats. "Dozens of cats, corpses everywhere," Mum remembers. "Their poor little poisoned bodies piled up in heaps, swelling in the sun. If you'd put them tip to tail, they would have gone all the way around the school buildings. And the next day we were overcome by the awful stench of burned fur and flesh when the gardeners doused them in fuel and set fire to them. It was too awful. Too, too wicked."

Mum considers that the nuns became bloodless and heartless because they weren't allowed to drink and gamble or have any fun, while the priests were allowed to get drunk and bet on horses at the racetrack. "The nuns were supposed to be above all earthly desires and temptations. They weren't even allowed to be observed eating. They had a furtive dining room at the back of school where they had to eat behind closed doors and closed curtains. No one could ever see them do anything biological. We school-children had an ongoing argument about whether or not nuns really did eat, and if they did, what happened at the other end. Of course, I think they took all their irritation and disappointments and repressed urges out on us."

After four years at the school, Mum had a fairly good idea that hell involved nuns and convents, so when an inferno worthy of Hades exploded in the blue gum trees near the school, it was not a surprise, but what *was* a shock was that Suk, as usual, was tethered to one of the trees. It was toward the end of the long dry season; the wind had been red all day with dust blown in from Uganda and settling on everything like powdered blood, the sun blistered out of a high, clear sky. Finally at noon that day, the volatile eucalyptus sap caught fire. From her desk in the classroom, Mum saw the flames out of the corner of her eye and was in a full run toward her donkey before her mind fully understood what her body already knew. But before she could run into the flames, she was caught fast in the powerful grip of Sister Philip's manly hands.

"I could feel the explosion of those trees in the pit of my stomach," Mum says. One tree after the other blew up, each flaring limb and trunk bringing the fire closer and closer to Suk. The little donkey tugged and strained at his halter, but the rope held fast. Mum watched helplessly as a wall of fire consumed the tree under which Suk fretted. The donkey disappeared from sight and his screams were lost in the roar of the oily flames. Mum felt the world contract into the denial that comes with tragedy, the refusal to believe that time cannot be stopped, reversed, undone. "No! No! No!"

Then, out of the flames, singed and braying in pain and fright, the donkey staggered, flesh and fur hanging from his back in charred strips. His halter rope had burned through, and was dangling under his chin. Mum tried to squirm out of Sister Philip's grip, but the woman's hands only squeezed tighter.

"Let me go!" Mum cried. She twisted and kicked in the vice of Sister Philip's grasp, but she could not get free. Then she swiveled her head and looked up at the nun and what she saw chilled her then, and stayed with her forever. "Sister Philip was staring at Suk with furious, cold blue eyes under her bushy ginger eyebrows. I knew then that she had put the Evil Eye on him. She'd started that fire." Mum nods. "I've never had any doubt about it. That bloody nun was a witch."

My grandmother nursed the donkey back to health with liquid paraffin and May & Baker antibiotic powders, but Suk sensibly refused to go anywhere near the school again. Anyway, he remained completely bald over much of his body, "and you can't ride a bald donkey." So for some months Mum was forced to walk to school every morning alone, and when she was sent to sit under the scorched eucalyptus trees, she could no longer lounge on the back of her donkey, staring up at the sky. Belatedly, and to her heartbroken surprise, she found she missed Suk's obstinate, scheming companionship.

The short November rains came, followed by the startled, green days of Christmas. Then the longer rains arrived in March and stayed all through May. Walking to school, Mum collected clogs of mud on the bottom of her shoes. The roads turned fluid and my grandfather had to put chains on his tires to drive anywhere. Then May dried into June and the long dry season started again.

"What you saw first," Mum says of the occasional, almost mystical arrival of the Somali horsemen, "was a pillar of dust coming from the edge of the plateau." And by nightfall they were in Eldoret and you could hear the bells around the necks of the lead mares and the men shouting to one another in their exotic desert tongue. Their little campfires lit orange out of the grasslands, and the shapes of horses milling and men in silhouette ghosted the vlei.

Hundreds of Somali ponies had arrived, worn muscular and sinewy having trekked almost the entire breadth of Kenya from the drylands of Somalia. "Only the fittest, sturdiest animals survived that long, difficult journey," Mum says. The herdsmen — every bit as tough as the animals they had come to sell — were lean and secretive behind their white wrappings of desert garb, dry and folded as moths.

Within the week, the horses were all taken over to Betty Webster's place, one of Eldoret's riding teachers. "She set up benches and a thatched shelter at her riding arena and there was an auction of all these fabulous ponies which, of course, I had to miss because of school. But my mother and father went. They were very keen on Somali ponies and they decided that a pony of my own was exactly what I needed to take my mind off what had happened to poor Suk."

Back in the early 1930s, before Thoroughbreds made it to East Africa, my grandfather had won the Kenya Gold Cup on his Somali pony, Billy. "Not much to look at," Mum says. "They tended to be ewe necked, goose rumped, straight in the shoulder, and they were tiny — average height, about thirteen point two hands — but the main thing is they had endurance and they could run like the wind if they felt like it."

At the auction, my grandmother was taken with a sturdy gray gelding. She thought he had a nice direct way of looking at a person. A herdsman with sun-baked eyes and a lip full of khat agreed to let her ride the pony before she bought it. For the first and only time in his life, the creature behaved like an angel. He allowed his feet and teeth to be checked, he didn't kick or bite, he willingly jumped every obstacle put in his path, he turned and halted nicely. My grandmother paid the herdsman a handsome sum and she named the pony Nane, Kiswahili for the large eight branded on his rump.

"He never went forward again," Mum says. "His only interest in life was food, which I suppose was understandable given he'd been on desert rations all his life until then." Every morning before school, my grandfather galloped his Thoroughbred mare, Vanity, out on the racetrack and Mum trailed behind on Nane. "The racetrack had been where the Italian prisoners of war camps were, so there were lots of overgrown and collapsed latrines that you had to be careful not to fall down. Otherwise, it was a perfect place for a morning gallop."

Nane hated his morning gallop. "He saw it as an unnecessary interruption in an otherwise perfect day of resting and eating," Mum says. He had a special trick of swelling himself up before beginning to buck, such inventive, furious twists and leaps that Mum was always dashed to the ground. "I could feel his neck puffing up and I'd start to shout, 'He's making his neck fat, he's making his neck fat,' and then he'd plunge and coil and I'd go airborne and hit the ground. But of course, with the minimum amount of fuss, I'd dust myself off and get back on again as soon as I could see straight. Then I'd ride to school, usually a bit battered and shaken. The nuns got angry with my father and said that I couldn't learn anything if I'd been knocked out two or three times before breakfast, but I think they were just lousy teachers."

The nuns organized games in the afternoon at the convent and tournaments of various kinds on the weekends. "Hours and hours of tedious tennis," Mum says. "But I never waited around long enough to hit a single ball." Instead, she took riding lessons. "To begin I rode with Babs Owens. She had a very scary, vicious temper. She was famous for flinging herself off a horse if it was annoying her and biting it as hard as she could on the ear." Babs would make Mum ride very rigidly, pressing a penny between her knees and the saddle. "If I dropped the penny — smack, biff, wallop — there was hell to pay." Mum sniffs. "Babs's husband, Cyril, had been a Japanese prisoner of war. And I'm sure that can't have been much fun, but I imagine it was a welcome break from a life of domestic bliss with Babs."

Then Babs's temper must have become too much because my grandparents shifted Mum's lessons over to Betty Webster. "I adored Betty," Mum says. "I think she was like a lot of Kenyan women of that time.

She marched around in corduroys and a man's shirt, very self-sufficient, very tough and independent and always trailed by a herd of dogs." Nane didn't improve much, but Mum's love of riding swelled beyond measure. "I can't separate horses from my childhood, or Betty Webster from my love of horses," she says. Mum holds up her hands and makes a pair of horse's ears with her fingers. "For as long as I can remember, I have seen the world from between the ears of a horse. That's my view. Straight ahead, don't look down. Don't look back."

About a year after she got him, Mum entered Nane into a show-jumping competition at the Eldoret Agricultural Show. "I think we managed to scramble over about three jumps, but the moment there was a suggestion of a spread, he dug his heels in, made his neck fat and then gave all the spectators their money's worth in an unscheduled rodeo. Still, I was expected to leave the arena smiling pleasantly."

The afternoon of Mum's humiliating defeat at the spread, Betty Webster rode her favorite gelding in the stadium event. "Around she went in beautiful form, sailing over everything. Then right in front of the grandstand there was a very tricky gate. Betty must have miscalculated the distance, or messed up her approach, because the gelding hit the jump in such a way he flipped right over it, head over heels, and landed on top of Betty." Mum describes the expanding stillness of the moments that followed. Everyday noises were unnaturally amplified — the hadeda ibis calling from the racetrack, horses shouting to one another from the collecting ring. "Then Betty's gelding scrambled to his feet, but Betty continued to lie there, very pale and still. She wasn't dead, but she was unconscious and you could tell from the way she was lying at such an unnatural angle that she'd broken her neck."

The riderless horse, reins slack around his legs, galloped away toward the arena gate, leaving the crumpled rider in the wreck of the jump. Someone ran out and grabbed the horse. A few others scrambled over the fence and ran toward Betty. She was loaded into the back of a car and driven off to the hospital. "One young man — I don't remember his name now — took her gelding," Mum says, "and bravely finished the round for her. He might have been shaking like a leaf, but he did it. Then he went on and rode the gelding for the rest of the weekend. The show *must* go on; we all understood that." Mum pauses. "That young fellow won on Betty's gelding, so on Sunday night, he took the cup to the hospital and put it on the pillow by her head. She never regained consciousness."

Betty's coffin was put on a large old ox cart. All her dogs were loaded up and sat among piles and piles of garlands. The cart was pulled by two black Percherons to the churchyard. "It was very tragic of course," Mum says, "but we thought it was a very right and proper ending for Betty."

Mum thinks for a moment. What she says next confirms for me what I've always known about her without ever having had the words to put into this knowledge. In her view, the immediate peril of a situation is always weighed against the glamorous obituary that might be written if the thing killed you: "I suppose that's why I've never seen the dangerous side of riding. For me it was always a brave and gallant sport, and if it did you in, it was a glorious way to go."

Nicola Fuller of Central Africa Goes to Her High School Reunion

Mum and Dad, newly engaged. Kenya, 1964.

When I was a child, Mum presented Kenya to me as a place of such forbidding perfection that its flawlessness shattered in the telling and what I was left holding on to were shards of equatorial light. Even the hinted-at, subsurface revolutionary tactics of the Mau Mau fighters, who were agitating for independence from British rule, were part of the romance. Kenya, in Mum's telling, was a land of such sepia loveliness, such fecundity, such fulfillment that it was *worth* dying for if you were white (if you were black and you wanted to die for Kenya, that was another matter altogether. Then you were an unpleasant, uppity Kikuyu anarchist). Mum made it clear that leaving Kenya was one of the great shocks of her life. "I never thought I would leave," she says. "I had such a magical childhood, filled with such magical people."

When I was sixteen, I read James Fox's *White Mischief.* The book is an account of the infamous Happy Valley set, a group of aristocratic flappers who came out to Kenya between the two world wars, shot lots of animals, behaved very badly and died in hedonistic droves. Hunting accidents, plane crashes and drugs and alcohol killed a fair number of them. Murder, venereal disease and suicide took a few more, and the whole disgraceful party teetered on January 24, 1941, with the discovery that the thirty-nine-year-old Josslyn Hay, Twenty-second Earl of Erroll, had been shot on the Nairobi-Ngong road after a decade of scandal, divorces, affairs and dalliances.

Notables of the Happy Valley set included Sir Jock Delves Broughton, Alice and Frédéric de Janzé, Lady Idina Sackville, Diana Caldwell, Jack Soames, John Carbery and Kiki Preston, none of whom I had ever heard of. I asked if these were the magical people of Mum's miraculous childhood. She shook her head and her eyes went pale. "The Happy Valley set were *not* us. No, they were very careless, very irresponsible and very boring. Nothing like us at all."

"I thought you said Kenyan people were so fun and interesting," I said.

"Not that lot," Mum said.

"How were you different?"

Mum looked as if I'd beaten her up with a dead fish. "In every way," she said. "We were *pukka*-pukka sahibs. They were cruel and silly. Wastrels." And then my mother took a deep breath. "I'll tell you an awful story about that lot," she said. "A really shocking story."

Mum and I were sitting at the veranda at the German-owned farm in Mkushi, Zambia, to which we had moved in the mid-1980s. It was the end of the dry season, not long after I had finished reading the James Fox book. The air was stung with the salty scent of burning msasa from forest fires. Dad had started plowing in preparation for the spring rains and dust from the fields added to the forest-fire smoke to create a yellow-gray sky. A mob of cows were wandering up from the dip, bellyaching for their calves. The herdsmen whistled and shouted, "Ha! Ha!" Our stubborn, rearing, bucking, biting bush ponies were grazing placidly in the home paddocks. A large yellow sun was making its way toward the hills in Zaire. I remember details like this because the story Mum told me that late afternoon was the first time I felt that the tranquil homeliness of Zambia was far preferable to Kenya's thrilling glamour.

"Shortly after my mother arrived in Kenya from Scotland, she took a position with a wealthy white hunter from the Happy Valley set," Mum said. "The white hunter, Inky Porter, was rich and spoiled, but I wouldn't say that she was an aristocrat." Mum looked disapproving. "*Aristocrat* implies good breeding, noblesse oblige." Mum sniffed to demonstrate that Inky Porter's behavior fell well short of the mark. "Anyway, this awful Inky Porter had found herself inconvenienced with a pregnancy right in the middle of the hunting season, so she hired my mother to help with the baby."

"Your mother was a nanny for Inky Porter," I clarified.

Mum blinked. "No, no, no," she said. "Nanny doesn't sound right."

We went back and forth for some time on a suitable noun. I suggested maid or child minder.

"No," Mum said. "She was more than that."

"Nurse?" I tried.

"No, she wasn't a nurse."

I attempted governess and au pair, but Mum refused them too. The way I looked at it, there was no getting around the fact that my grandmother was a nanny. The way Mum looked at it, I didn't understand class at all. "Don't forget, my mother was from a very good family," she reminded me. "She would not have been simply a nanny."

So my grandmother was a not-simply-a-nanny for a not-worthy-to-be-called-an-aristocrat white hunter named Inky Porter. "And Inky Porter," Mum said, "liked to drink gallons of gin and sniff mountains of cocaine. She was a big fan of adultery and intrigues, and she was very bored with the idea of children. So the moment her baby was born, Inky Porter handed it over to my mother, then she pushed off to Uganda to shoot lots of animals, drink gallons of cocktails and generally make up for lost time. But the poor baby was born absolutely pickled in gin and withdrawing from cocaine. It was awful. The infant died in agony — seizures, fevers, tremors — in my mother's arms when it was only a few days old."

For a while Mum and I stared silently into the empty space held by Inky Porter's dead baby. "And that is why I am so impatient with all this celebration of that Happy Valley crowd," Mum concluded. "All these books and films and carry-on that make their lives seem so glamorous. No one talks about the poor dead baby." Then Mum spoke slowly, for emphasis and so that I would never again make the mistake of muddling up her — or any of her family — with the Happy Valley set. "We didn't live like that in Eldoret. We were surrounded by *pukka*-pukka sahibs, proper gentry. People like Betty Webster and Zoe Foster — good, wholesome, outdoorsy types."

Everyone Mum knew had lots of dogs and horses. They all played cricket or rugby twice a week and went for long, improving walks every evening. On the weekends, the whole community show-jumped or entered gymkhanas and raced their ponies. "Which was quite exhausting and didn't leave much energy for too much funny nonsense," Mum said. And once or twice a month, the district dressed up at amateur theatricals, sang naughty songs and satisfied the very British need to see men in drag. "We had lots and lots of good, clean fun," Mum said.

When I was in my final year of high school in Zimbabwe, Vanessa took a year off doing very little for a television show in London (a sign above her desk asked the really very good question, "What DOES Vanessa do?") and backpacked around Africa on trains and buses, by boat and by foot. When she came home — sunburned and much thinner as a result of being too vague and polite to refuse any food offered to her no matter how long it had been sitting out in the sun smothered in flies and thereby spending much of her year trying to find clean loos in remote places — I peppered her with questions about Kenya. Had she seen Mum's childhood home? Was the light perfect? Had she met any *pukka*-pukka sahibs? But Vanessa had frustratingly little to say on the matter of Kenya. She had gone as far as Nakuru to see the hospital in which she had been born and then she had spent a fortnight on the coast in a cheap hotel that turned out to be a brothel.

"There were people knocking on the door all night," she said. " 'Kissy-kissy five shillings.' "

"How fascinating," I said.

"Oh goodness," Vanessa said, "you're just like Great-Uncle Dicken." She shut her eyes.

"No it wasn't fascinating. It was yuck."

I left home, married and moved to Wyoming with my American husband. I got on with the business of raising children and I wrote the Awful Book. For the first time in my life, I had the opportunity to go to Kenya and see the place for myself, but there didn't seem much point in going without Mum, and Mum was barely talking to me, let alone agreeing to family holidays. Then, two years after the Awful Book was published, Auntie Glug had a mania-induced brainstorm to attend her high school reunion in Kenya. She called to tell me about her plan and to ask me if I knew Mum and Dad's phone number in Zambia.

"You'll have to write them a letter," I said. "They haven't answered their phone in months."

"Typical," Auntie Glug said.

"I think it's because of the Awful Book," I said.

"Yes, well," Auntie Glug said.

"I want to go to your reunion," I said.

"You're not an old girl," Auntie Glug objected.

"I'm oldish," I said.

I could hear Auntie Glug taking a long drag off her cigarette.

"Please, Auntie," I begged.

"Well if you're going to be a tag-along Niece-Weevil," Auntie Glug said, "I'll leave it up to you to get your mum and dad to come along too."

But from the very start, Nicola Fuller of Central Africa was not keen on the whole idea of the reunion: "Not really my sort of thing." She made a face. "They'll all be pretending they're so thrilled to see someone to whom they haven't given a second thought in forty years."

We had been sitting under the Tree of Forgetfulness on my parents' fish and banana farm in the middle Zambezi valley for the better part of a mediocre box of South African wine. I was trying to be persuasive and nonchalant at the same time, attempting to appeal to Mum's highly developed sense of adventure without arousing her extraordinarily overdeveloped sense of mistrust (which had been on code red since the publication of the Awful Book). She took a sip of wine. "And another thing," she said. "They'll all have read the Awful Book and they'll be counting my drinks. I'll resent that."

"Maybe they'll be drunk themselves," I tried.

Mum ignored me. "Or they'll go on and on about how happy and smiling all the locals are." Her brow sank over the rim of her wineglass. "Well, of course the locals are always smiling — that's the expression least likely to arouse suspicion."

I was running out of arguments. "Well, it *was* the school you liked," I said.

This, at least, was true. A reunion at the convent would have been out of the question, but this was a reunion of the Highlands School to which Mum and Auntie Glug had gone after leaving the convent. Unlike the convent, the Highlands School offered a decent education, a good art teacher, and, all things considered, Mum wasn't unhappy during her four years there. "That doesn't mean I want to sit around with a bunch of old girls talking about it," she said with a shudder.

But Auntie Glug's manic episode persisted and by September, the whole fixture had been organized. Old girls had been rounded up from all over Britain, and rooms had been arranged at the Nyali Beach Hotel in Mombasa ("Oh dear," Mum said, "they'll have sticky drinks and so-called traditional dancers to greet us, all ululating and carrying on"). There was to be an evening excursion on the Indian Ocean in a dhow

("There go half the Old Girls' wallets," Mum predicted), an opportunity to wander the streets of Old Arab Town ("There go the other half"). Finally, there was to be a plane ride up to Nairobi for a night at the Muthaiga Country Club ("All those pretentious ex-pats playing pukka sahib on the lawn"), followed by a day in a snake park and a safari in the Masai Mara. (Mum shut her eyes. "No," she said. "I have elephants in the bananas, crocodiles in the ponds and hippos in the garden anytime I want. I don't think so.")

Nevertheless, the following February, we all arrived at the Nyali Beach Hotel — a dozen Old Girls from the Eldoret Highlands School, Mum, Dad, Uncle Sandy, Auntie Glug (whose mania had worn itself out on a walk across the Brazilian rain forest and had now resolved itself into a gentle depression) and me. Our taxi stopped outside a sturdy cement barrier while a guard crawled around with a mirror to check its undercarriage for ordnance.

Eighteen months earlier, a red sports utility vehicle had crashed through the gardens and barrier outside the Paradise Hotel, the only Israeli-owned hotel in Mombasa. Sixty Israeli tourists had just checked in and were enjoying their welcome sticky drink. When the vehicle hit the lobby, it had exploded, killing two Israeli children, one Israeli adult and nine Kenyan traditional dancers. Almost simultaneously, two shoulder-launched Strela-2 surface-to-air missiles were fired at an Israeli-based Arkia Airlines Boeing 757 as it took off from Moi International Airport in Mombasa, barely missing the aircraft. Kenya's security was still in the process of being thoroughly assessed.

And Kenya's security was increasingly suspicious of Mum. "Hujambo, askari!" she told the security guard. "Pole sana. Those horrible, vicious terrorists." She smiled magnificently and stuck her head out of the window and addressed the guard loudly. "The tourists will be back. You mustn't give up hope." The guard frowned nervously at Mum and asked the taxi driver to open the boot. "That's right," Mum said, encouragingly, "you must carry on. You must have courage." And then she broke into a long string of Swahili that she spoke deliberately and in incantations, as if wrapping a spell around Swahili speakers from which the rest of us were to be excluded.

Released from the uneasy security guard, we swept up to the hotel. The taxi driver jumped out and opened Mum's door. She paused a moment — as if her foot touching the earth might break the spell — before stepping out onto the gravel. She breathed in the salty, humid air and her arms went out in front of her. For one astonishing moment I thought she was going to embrace the taxi driver. Instead, she offered him her hands and he took them, helping her to her feet. They bantered back and forth in Swahili, a tongue in which Mum must be a stand-up comedienne because they had to prop each other up through gales of laughter.

At the reception, Mum sniffed and wiped her eyes when the traditional dancers came out to greet us. "Oh bravo," she said. "Well done!" When the dance was over she clapped enthusiastically and shouted, "Mzuri sana! Encore! Encore!" Her mood was infectious. The traditional dancers, surprised by such unbridled enthusiasm, began their dance again. "I'll take another one of those delicious sticky drinks," Mum said, swooping down on the woman holding the tray.

Dad filled in the guest registration card without his usual griping ("Good God, what are you trying to do, kill every last tree with all this bloody paperwork?"). Instead, in the space requesting "Please list all allergies," he caused hilarity by writing "WOMEN AND ALCOHOL." Then when he greeted the Old

Girls who were collecting against the reception desk he was so effusively warm and courtly that several of them retreated into the potted plants, their hats and money belts askew.

"Let's have a party!" Dad said, handing Auntie Glug a sticky drink. She propped herself up against an arrangement of wooden curios and looked as if she were beginning to have second thoughts about the reunion.

Meanwhile, Mum clapped along to the dancers, and cocked her hips this way and that. "Asante sana!" my mother cried. "And what beautiful voices, what lovely smiles you all have!" The traditional dancers trooped out into the sunshine with my mother cheering them on. In fact, she seemed in danger of joining them more or less permanently. "All right," Dad said, sensing how things might easily unravel, "that's enough for now, Tub." Then, in his enthusiasm to demonstrate that nearly forty years of marriage had done nothing to diminish his chivalry, he accidentally hit my mother in the head opening the door for her from the reception room into the garden. Mum reeled into the cannas clutching her eye.

Auntie Glug stared into her sticky drink. "I wonder how these go with Prozac?" she asked.

■ ■ ■ ■

Aside from our small party gathered for the Highlands School reunion and a group of American geologists who had been exploring for oil in Uganda, no one was staying at the hotel. Nor were any of the other hotels up and down the beach much occupied. A few rent boys combed the beach for old European women, but found only a couple of takers: an Italian matron of leathery complexion and a broken French woman in her early seventies with bad knees. Without the customary crowd of guests into which to fade, the old women seemed doubly desperate, and the rent boys looked doubly ill used. "Why on earth can't they go to bed with a good book like everyone else?" Mum asked, eyes lowered over a glass of cold Tusker.

Even beyond the main tourist strip everything still felt ghosted and shocked from the attack against the Paradise Hotel. Our Swahili guide, Mr. Faraji, gave us a tour of Fort Jesus and the spice market and he walked us through the old Arab quarters, but it was as if a disease had washed over the place, taking with it the usual, pushy, vibrant clatter of an ancient port city. "Oh dear," Mum said, "how sad and quiet."

"Very quiet and sad," Mr. Faraji agreed.

So Mum and Mr. Faraji embarked on a two-person mission to revive Mombasa. Nothing could dim their excitement, their curiosity, or their determination to be deeply impressed by everything. Mum bought spices and kikois, baskets and carvings, beads and postcards while Mr. Faraji haggled with hawkers to secure her the best price. Mum admired every angle of the city, ran her fingers along the woodwork on the doors, joked with the shopkeepers and bought food from everyone who offered it to her even though Mr. Faraji begged her not to eat anything from street vendors.

"Why ever not?" Mum said, licking her fingers.

I reassured Mr. Faraji that Mum is an extreme omnivore. She has eaten snails peeled off the farm's driveway and wild frogs' legs from the bush surrounding the Tree of Forgetfulness. Once she even ate a prawn cocktail in hyperlandlocked, socialist-era Zambia, and if that didn't kill her, I argued, a little dysentery-laced street food in Mombasa wasn't going to do the trick.

While we walked through the Old Arab quarter, Mr. Faraji tried to give us each a sprig of fragrant wild marigold to hold to our noses. Mum shook her head. "Oh no," she said. "I'd be very offended if someone walked past my house sniffing herbs." She stepped over a broken, bubbling pipe. "And I'm sure my drains smell at least as bad as this."

One afternoon, Mr. Faraji took us out to a beach near the harbor. This was the site of the children's holiday camp where the Huntingfords had stayed for three weeks every year. We all piled out of the taxi. There was no sign of the holiday resort now, but there was a hot little shack on the edge of a littered beach to which we all repaired. There was a smell of sewage and rotting fish. An unfinished concrete building sprouted rusting rebar. "Now," Mum said, half closing her eyes, "this was where we spent our glorious holidays."

By some miracle, Mr. Faraji managed to procure some cold beers for all of us, so we sat in the tin shack while Mum repainted the dreary beach as it had been in her glorious childhood. Another round of cold beer arrived on the heels of the last and the sun began its slow descent over the land so that the sea became a tranquil sheet of gold. As Mum remembered it, the holiday camp at Mombasa was almost unmitigated bliss — watching the huge ships pull into the harbor, diving for shells, exploring empty beaches, swimming in the shark fence (which may explain why Mum always swims with her head well above water, as if scanning the horizon for fins). The only drawback to these holidays seemed to have been the ablution block. "It was very off-putting. There was one large building for men and one large building for women, and in the women's bathroom, there were eight holes all lined up next to one another without any divisions over one huge pit." Mum shook her head at the memory. "*Very* hard to relax."

Our days took on a predictable rhythm resolving into a pleasant routine. In the morning, we were awakened by the rhythmic scraping of the gardener's broom against the sandy walkways and the shouting mynah birds. Afternoons brought camels strolling up the beach and heat-stunned siestas under the umbrellas around the pool. In the evenings, stars appeared slowly over the Indian Ocean, the Guiana chestnut slapped against the windows in the breeze, and a dense peace settled against the hotel. The heavy air was thick with frangipani, tropical lilies and gardenia. "Everything's changed everywhere," Mum said. "But some things here feel very familiar. Wonderful people, gorgeous gardens, exciting markets, delicious spices and so much more ancient feeling than anywhere else I've been in Africa, such *culture,* such diversity. Oh, I shall always be a child of Kenya, always."

After supper, Mum, Dad, Auntie Glug and Uncle Sandy created a dance floor in the hotel restaurant. By ten or eleven most evenings, we seemed to be the only people awake on the whole beach and we trailed our small party out onto the sand. Then, dancing together in the moonlight, Mum and Dad appeared as they must have in their twenties: beautiful, optimistic and aware of being the most exciting couple anyone had ever met.

The barman put on Doris Day and Mum moved into Dad's arms. "Gonna take a sentimental journey," Mum and Doris sang together. "Gonna set my heart at ease." Then my parents danced close to the bar and I could smell her perfume, his pipe tobacco. "Gonna make a sentimental journey, to renew old memories." Mum sank back against Dad's shoulder briefly before spinning back out into the shadows. Even in the near dark I could see a crescent of tears brimming in Mum's eyes. "Got my bag, got my reservations," she sang along. "Spent each dime I could afford. . . . Gotta take that sentimental journey, sentimental journey home."

I turned back to the bar and sighed. "Go on, Niece-Weevil," Auntie Glug said, pushing a sticky drink toward me. "One of these can't hurt."

NICOLA HUNTINGFORD, THE AFRIKANER AND THE PERFECT HORSE

Circa 1957

Mum and Violet. Kenya, circa 1958.

Sometimes memory does a trick of packaging events together so that they are conveniently conflated and easier to retrieve. In this way, Mum remembers nothing of the circus that came through Eldoret in the mid-1950s except that Nane left with it. "I suppose my mother must have thought that he had knocked me out one too many times," she says, "so off he went to feed the lions." Mum gives a little gulp. "And I don't know if this is the way I imagined it, or if this really happened, but I have a picture in my head of Nane bouncing off down the road behind bars, peering back at me, with big pleading eyes."

"Oh, that's awful," I say.

Mum thinks about this for a moment. "Yes, it was," she says. Then she looks uncomfortable and I can tell she does not want to seem like an ungrateful Christopher-bloody-Robin type. So she clears her throat and revises the story, assuming a stiff upper lip for the task. "Well," she says, "I'm sure my parents didn't tell me he was going to feed the lions at the time. I am sure they told me that Nane had run away to join the circus. Trapeze artists, dancing bears, happy days."

My grandparents asked knowledgeable friends to source a really good replacement for Nane. In their minds, they pictured a Thoroughbred, something largehearted and bold that could match my Mum's courage and skill in the show-jumping arena. Golden Duckling, the horse the friends selected, was very well bred by King Midas out of Cold Duck. "She was a great big Thoroughbred,"

Mum says, "pretty head, nice neck, she was perfectly put together until you got to her legs." Mum pauses from dramatic effect. "They were sawed off."

I look suitably horrified.

"I know," Mum says. "We all stood in the stable yard in Nairobi staring at this apparition, but we were too polite to tell the friends who were supposed to be experts that they had selected a dud. Sawed-off legs *and* curved hocks" — Mum turns her elbows out in an impression of a horse with bad conformation — "which meant she'd just fall down in the middle of whatever you were doing. Oh," she adds, "and she had an absolutely murderous disposition."

Nevertheless Mum — brought up by her parents not to complain almost no matter what — gamely paid forty pounds of her own money for the horse (more than half a century later she remembers with undiminished resentment the exact amount), and the thing was hauled home in the back of a truck. "Well, Duckling wasn't ideal," Mum admits. "In fact she was pretty awful, but she was what I had." So Mum entered show-jumping competitions as before, and as before she contributed significantly to everyone's entertainment. "I usually left the arena unconscious, strapped to a stretcher, dripping blood," she says with a happy smile.

For a year or two the homicidal, sawed-off Thoroughbred bashed Mum senseless week after week and Mum gamely hauled herself back onto the creature for more punishment. And then — beginning in the year Mum turned thirteen — an almost biblical series of events brought her Violet, a horse of such shining perfection that none of the scores of other horses she has owned since have ever quite rivaled that one, flawless animal.

"In 1957, there were terrific floods in Eldoret," Mum says. "Water roared down the passageway, the choo was submerged, the cows and horses stood around up to their knees in mud, the roads washed away, the mud bricks on all the buildings got soggy, the walls sagged, the roof leaked, the laundry never dried, frogs moved into the house." This went on for weeks and by the time the sun did come out again, the community was very run-down and measles broke out. "It started in the villages, then the old ladies next door got sick, then half the kids in my school got sick plus all the nuns. Then the Polish refugees keeled over and finally my father caught it," Mum says.

My grandfather had to lie in a darkened room for a couple of months. "Doctor Reynolds told him not to read, but of course he did and ruined his eyesight forever." And my grandmother was run ragged taking care of sick people. She took meat and milk to the Nandi villages; she ferried soup and bread up to the old ladies. She visited the sick boarding-school children and took clean linens to the nuns. She fed the Polish refugees — "Eldoret was smothered in them for some reason," Mum says, "and they all insisted they were princesses and counts. Very unlikely, I would have said" — and finally she came back to bathe my grandfather's rash in calamine lotion and give him his supper.

One morning, into this overwrought and distracted atmosphere, Flip Prinsloo arrived at the Huntingford's door, the brim of his sweat-stained felt hat clutched in his fists, and asked to see Mrs. Huntingford. My grandmother ordered tea from the drunken Cherito and sat out on the veranda with Flip. It says something about my grandmother — and about Flip, for that matter — that the two of them waited for the tea tray to arrive in perfectly companionable silence. It also says something about the depth of Flip's desperation that he had come to a British woman for help. "You see," Mum explains, "in Eldoret, there was a big group of very British settlers, like our family. And then there was a quite big group of very Afrikaner settlers, like Flip. And of course the two groups did not mix at all." Mum narrows her eyes. "The Boer War," she says darkly. "Never, ever forget the Boer War, Bobo. They certainly haven't."

The Dutch arrived in South Africa at the Cape of Good Hope, on the southwestern tip of Africa, in 1652. To begin with, they saw themselves not as settlers but as temporary workers, there to grow vegetables for the Dutch East India Company's ships sailing between Holland and Indonesia. But by the early 1700s, independent trekboers — nomadic farmers — had broken away from the Dutch East India Company and were pushing into the wild, pepper-scented land to the north, displacing the native Khoikhoi. Over time, these trekboers began to call themselves Afrikaners (Africans) to mark their sense of a new identity as distinct and separate from the Dutch. And they developed a distinct language — Afrikaans — basic Dutch salted with whatever other languages were floating around the Cape at that time. In 1795, the British, looking to protect their sea routes and alarmed by the empire-building intentions of other European countries, sent an expedition to the Cape and easily forced the Dutch to surrender, but they hadn't counted on — or recognized — the increasingly cohesive and nationalistic sensibilities of the Afrikaners. By the mid 1830s, British rule had so disgusted the Afrikaners (the 1834 emancipation of slaves was the final straw) that about twelve thousand of them responded by emigrating far into the interior — the Great Trek, it was called afterward — and setting up two of their own independent Afrikaner-run republics, the Orange Free State and the Transvaal.

War is Africa's perpetual ripe fruit. There is so much injustice to resolve, such desire for revenge in the blood of the people, such crippling corruption of power, such unseemly scramble for the natural resources. The wind of power shifts and there go the fruit again, tumbling toward the ground, each war more inventively terrible than the last. In 1880, the British confiscated a Boer's wagon because he had not paid his taxes. Needing nothing but the smallest of excuses, the Boers retaliated by declaring war against the British. Within a year, the British had been defeated. The Afrikaners would later call this their First War of Independence. The British would call it the First Anglo-Boer War.

But the subsequent gold rush of 1886 attracted even more British to the Boer republics. Never forgetting their resentment, the Afrikaners refused to let the British vote. Even by the 1890s, when there were more British than Afrikaners in the republics, the Afrikaners denied the British the vote. This provoked the Second Anglo-Boer War, or what the Afrikaners called the Second War of Freedom, in October 1899. This time the British took no chances. Four hundred fifty thousand soldiers came to South Africa from Britain, Australia, New Zealand and Canada to fight fewer than sixty thousand Boers. This time the war was longer and even more excessively nasty and brutish than the last.

Although the Afrikaners had no official army, they had been on the continent for two centuries and they had the land in their blood (to say nothing of their blood in the land). They needed no barracks or uniforms, and no generals to give them orders. They had sturdy horses, strong men and tenacious women. Their children were crack shots, raised to be tough and self-sufficient. On the other hand, the British troops wore impractical red jackets that shone out of the blond high veldt like stoplights. They didn't understand the language of this wide, sad land, nor did they love it. The only way they could win the war was backhandedly — by starving and diseasing the Afrikaners out of existence. So between 1901 and 1902, the British scorched more than thirty thousand farms and placed almost all the Afrikaner women and children in the world's first concentration camps. As many as twenty-nine thousand Boers died from the appalling conditions in those camps; so did twenty thousand blacks who had been caught working on Boer farms. By the time a peace treaty was signed at the town of Vereeniging on May 21, 1902, the British army had killed nearly one quarter of all the Boers in existence.

Flip Prinsloo had come to Kenya as a baby with his parents and forty-seven other Afrikaner families from the Transvaal. The families were mostly bywoners (poor tenant farmers who had no hope of purchasing land of their own) or hensoppers (those who had surrendered to the British during the Boer War and who now found the shame of that surrender unbearable). Both the bywoners and the hensoppers wanted a large piece of free, unoccupied African land on which to settle. The last thing they wanted — having done little else in living memory — was to have to fight or die for that land. "But there it was and they were welcome to it," Mum says. "No one else had settled there — too windy and far-flung for the tastes of most people."

The Uasin Gishu plateau on which the town of Eldoret now sits had been occupied in precolonial times first by the Sirikwa, then by the Masai and finally by the Nandi. In other words, the British considered it "unoccupied," a perceived emptiness that irked them. Consequently, they offered it to the Zionists as a temporary refuge for Russian Jews until a homeland in Israel could be established. But the Zionists rejected the offer, some of them weeping openly at the 1903 sixth Zionist Congress and quoting from Psalm 137, "How shall we sing the Lord's song in a strange land? If I forget thee, O Jerusalem, let my right hand forget her cunning. If I do not remember thee, let my tongue cleave to the roof of my mouth; if I prefer not Jerusalem above my chief joy."

So in semidesperation the British offered the land to British-abhorring Afrikaners from the Transvaal, and in 1908 more than two hundred Boers arrived by ship in Mombasa, Kenya. They took trains as far as Nakuru, where they purchased native oxen, which they trained to pull wagons all through the long rainy season of March, April and May. At the end of May, they began to climb from the Rift Valley, up the escarpment to their new homeland. It took them two months to cover one hundred miles, the wagons churning through mud up to the tops of their wheels and the forest dense and impassable in places. The trekkers cut bamboo to make causeways across swamps. The drivers stayed near the oxen, urging them step by slithering step.

In a wetland at the top of the escarpment a wagon loaded with sugar sank up to its axles and all the sugar melted. While the trekkers struggled for days to free the wagon, a two-year-old girl died of pneumonia. The young men planted poles and created a rudimentary sacred site for the funeral, and the Afrikaners grieved in the way of stoical people, tight lipped and moist eyed. They buried the girl in a place which they called Suiker Vlei — Sugar Vlei — and the next day they freed the wagon and continued the journey to the Sosiani River.

"There was at that time," Mum says, "a hunter called Cecil Hoey who lived on the other side of what would become Eldoret. He saw what he thought was a long stream of smoke snaking its way up the escarpment onto the highlands. And then he realized he was seeing the pale canvas of covered wagons winding up to the plateau. It was the trekkers arriving." Mum says, "Cecil took one look at that lot and predicted the end of the wildlife. He was right because when those Afrikaners first got there they had nothing to live off except what they could kill, and they finished off all the animals in no time."

The Afrikaners made harrows from branches and thorns bound with leather thongs made from zebra skin, they made soap from eland fat and they made shoes from the hides of giraffes. They ate what they could snare or shoot and they lived in grass-thatched houses made from their own mud bricks, baked in the high-altitude sun. "A lot of them were very basic," Mum says. "They weren't educated and they didn't read anything except the Bible. But they were tough and resourceful and they could live off nothing, those people." And then she sniffs and I can tell that it wounds her to make this next admission. "Well, that was *most* of them. But some of them were quite posh. One Afrikaner family was *so* posh that the Queen Mother stayed with them when she came to Kenya in 1959." Mum pauses to let me absorb this startling knowledge. "Imagine that," she says. "There's no way our shoddy little house would have been fit for royalty, but there they were — those posh Afrikaners — entertaining the Queen Mother!"

At last Cherito lurched onto the veranda with a tray of tea and a bottle of my grandmother's homemade wine.

"Thank you," my grandmother said.

Cherito staggered back into the kitchen. My grandmother's hand hovered over the tray. "Tea, Mr. Prinsloo?" she offered. "Or something a little stronger?"

Flip blinked.

My grandmother poured them both a glass of wine. "It burns a little at first," she warned, "but it's not bad once you get used to it." She took a sip of her wine. "Here's to us." She raised her glass. "There're none like us, and if there were, they're all dead."

Flip took a sip.

"What do you think?" my grandmother asked.

Flip's lips were stuck to his teeth, so he did not answer.

"Not bad, eh?" My grandmother poured herself another glass. "Mud in your eye," she said. The second glass tasted better than the first, and working off the theory that the third would therefore be better than the second, my grandmother gave herself another helping. "To absent friends!" she cried. Which was how, when Flip finally got

136

around to the reason for his visit, he found my grandmother in a pleasantly receptive mood.

"I've been watching your daughter riding," Flip said suddenly.

My grandmother narrowed her eyes at him. "Have you?"

"I like her style," he said. "Lots of blood."

"Well," my grandmother said, "I suppose that's one way of looking at it."

There was a long pause. Flip cleared his throat. "Dingaan's Day is coming up," he said.

Each year on December 16 Afrikaners everywhere celebrated Dingaan's Day. The most significant date in their calendar, it memorialized a battle in 1838 when a Voortrekker column defeated Dingaan's Zulu warriors on the banks of a river in modern-day KwaZulu-Natal. In Zulu they call that battle iMpi yaseNcome, the Battle of Ncome River. In Afrikaans they say it was Slag van Bloedrivier, the Battle of Blood River. But whatever you call it, the outcome was the same. On that day — with everything you can imagine going against them — four hundred seventy Voortrekkers roundly defeated tens of thousands of Zulu warriors. By nightfall, the Ncome River ran red with the blood of three thousand slain Zulus.

No Afrikaners were killed in the battle and only three were wounded. This proved, the Afrikaners said, that their tribe had a divine right to exist on South African land.

My grandmother sighed and looked with some regret at her empty wineglass. "So it is," she said. "How time flies."

Flip cleared his throat again. "I want to beat my cousin Pieter at the Dingaan Day races," he said.

My grandmother sat up. If there was one thing calculated to catch her interest, even through the fog of her homemade fig wine and lots of violent history, it was horse racing. "Is that so?"

"Yes," Flip said.

"Do you have a good horse?" My grandmother gave a little hiccup and wagged her finger at Flip. "That's the thing to win a race," she said. "A good horse."

"I've got a very good horse," Flip said. "But I need someone who will ride it. My sons. . . . Agh no, man." Flip put his head in his enormous hands. "They're no good." He looked at my grandmother, his eyes desperate. "I want your daughter."

My grandmother gave another hiccup.

"I'll pay her," Flip offered.

My grandmother looked horrified and flapped a hand at Flip. "No, no, no. Don't be silly." She hiccuped again. "You must have her for nothing. Free to good friends. Go ahead. Take her."

So the next afternoon, Flip Prinsloo came to the house and picked up Mum and drove her to his farm. "He had a bottle of South African brandy under his seat," Mum says, "and he'd take slurps out of it as we drove along. He offered me some, but I wasn't about to drink from a bottle that some scrubby old Afrikaner had been gulping out of." To make up for this, Flip bought my mother an enormous slab of chocolate when he stopped at the Venus Bar to replenish his brandy supply. "Which gave me spots," Mum warns. "So that was an important lesson. If someone offers you either brandy or chocolate, you should always take the brandy."

At the farm, Mum was left alone in a dimly lit sitting room while lunch was prepared. "All the furniture pressed against the skirting boards and a host of immensely chilling ancestors glared down from the walls," Mum says. Lunch was an awkward affair: "A very severe wife, a couple of hulking sons and one crushed-looking daughter-in-law." Except for the occasional outburst in Afrikaans, the family ate in silence. "I didn't understand what they said, but it certainly sounded as if they were plotting to kill me," she says.

Boiled mutton — "Grisly," Mum says — was followed by stewed coffee and fried sweetbreads, and then Flip reached for his sweat-stained hat and pushed himself away from the table. "Time to race," he said. The sons wiped their lips and stood up. They, too, reached for their veldskoen hats. "Kom," Flip told Mum.

The farm was on the edge of the plateau, and even though the Prinsloos had been cultivating it for fifty years, the buildings looked inadequate and hasty in the face of all the earth and sky they were trying to command. The place had a haunted feel, as if it were in mourning for its old self. From a rough-hewn livestock shed a syce emerged, leading three horses: two ordinary-looking geldings and a bay mare plunging at the end of her lead rope.

"Dit is jou perd," Flip told Mum. "Violet."

Mum was speechless.

"I'll never forget the first time I saw her," she says. "I don't think she ever had two feet on the ground at any one time. She wasn't tall but she had these long elegant legs, and a powerful chest. I could see, just looking at her, that she could run like the wind."

"Well," Flip said. "Op jou merka. First one to the end of the maize field wins."

140

Without warning and certainly without waiting for my mother, the Prinsloo sons leaped onto the two geldings and took off along the edge of a maize field. "Those Afrikaners didn't know how to train horses," Mum says. "They just put very savage bits in their mouths and rode like mad." Mum was still hopping about, trying to get her leg over the saddle, when Violet took off after the other horses.

"I don't know how I stayed on," Mum says. "But I did. I somehow managed to scramble up into the saddle with the mare at full gallop, grab the reins and hang on while she flew up the maize field. And I beat the sons, both of whom had tumbled down antbear holes long before the finish line."

That December, Mum won the Dingaan's Day race on Violet, outpacing Flip Prinsloo's cousin Pieter by lengths. Flip was drunk with victory. He bought Mum slabs and slabs of chocolate at the Venus Bar and he offered to marry her off to his sons. "One was about thirteen and the other was already married," Mum says. "But Flip said that didn't matter. He said I could have either, or both — whichever I wanted."

"I don't want your sons," Mum told Flip. She didn't want the chocolate either. She wanted Violet.

Flip shook his head. "No, not the horse," he said.

"If I can't have her, I won't ride her," Mum said.

Flip fingered his hat. "Is that so?"

"Yes," Mum said.

In the end, Mum and Flip struck a deal. She could borrow the horse all year for show jumping and hacking — anything she wanted — as long as she would ride for him every year on Dingaan's Day.

"Done," Mum said, shaking one of Flip Prinsloo's enormous hands.

Flip fetched the brandy bottle from under his seat and took a long swallow. "Op Violet," he said, offering Mum a sip.

Mum put the bottle to her lips. "To Violet," she agreed.

So for the first time in her life, Mum won everything she entered: show jumping, racing, bending poles. "That mare had one speed: flat out. No one could stop her. I couldn't stop her. But I could just about steer her and as long as I could stay on, we won, we won, we won. We won everything."

Nicola Huntingford and the Mau Mau

Donnie on the farm. Kenya, circa 1960.

Once a week my grandfather took Auntie Glug and Mum to one of the two movie theaters in Eldoret: either the Roxy or the Lyric. From one week to the next, Mum wallowed in the agreeable agony of having to choose between Rowan Tree fruit gums or Wilkinson's dolly mixture. "By the time we arrived at the cinema, I'd be half dead with indecision because they were all such beautiful sweets," she says. Then, having painstakingly selected the treats, Mum, Auntie Glug and my grandfather were shown to their seats by ushers who were dressed up like organ-grinders' monkeys in funny little uniforms with fezzes perched on the side of their heads.

The lights went down and, through the backlit mauve-gray gauze of cigarette smoke, the show began. First, a Pathé News reel, a jingoistic British production that always included something cheerful for the far-flung subjects. "The royal family doing something horsey or a factory in Manchester belching lots of patriotic smoke into a gloomy English sky," Mum says. After the news, there was a pause while the adults refreshed their cocktails and the Indians who ran the movie theater sweated over the ancient, dust-rusted projection machines.

"Finally, after much ado, the main event," Mum says. "Usually a war movie with lots of wicked Nazis coming to a sticky end and heroic British soldiers prevailing against overwhelming evil. The sound system was awful, so we struggled if they showed a Western because we couldn't understand their accents." Mum gives me a reproachful look as if I were personally responsible for the shortcomings of John Wayne's elocution. Then she continues in a more conciliatory tone. "Although their plots were very simple, of course, so it didn't matter too much — a bunch of cowboys wiping out bunches and bunches of Indians." Mum sniffs. "Very hard on their horses, we always thought."

She and I are having this conversation while driving north from Cape Town to Clanwilliam in the Western Cape, having rendezvoused for a holiday in South Africa. I have come from Wyoming and Mum and Dad have flown from Zambia to meet me. It is the end of the cold rainy season, and the air outside is humming in anticipation of the ferocious heat of summer, which is gathering strength, moment by moment. Each day begins with a memory of chill, but by noon baking waves are rocking the ground. Mum looks out the window, but I can tell she isn't seeing the citrus farms, neatly laid out like strung jewels on pale sandy soil along the Olifants River, nor is she seeing the ash-purple fynbos that smothers the flanks of the mountains here. In her head, Mum is back in Eldoret, in a stuffy, smoke-filled cinema and it is the early 1950s.

"And of course they never forgot the national anthem," Mum says dreamily, putting her hand over her heart. "Every show

145

they played 'God Save the King' — or 'God Save the Queen,' whoever it was — and you had to leap to your feet respectfully, God save our gracious Queen, long live our noble Queen. God Save the Queen!" Mum is singing softly, "La la la la! Send her victorious, happy and glorious, Tra la la la la la laaa la la! God save the Queen."

She resumes her speaking voice and says with pride, "Did you know that Princess Elizabeth was actually in Kenya when her father died?"

"Yes," I say.

"Did you?" Mum's voice expresses doubt that I could really know such a wonderfully imperialistic fact. "Yes, well, she and Phil were staying at the Tree-tops Lodge in the Aberdares in February 1952." Mum's eyes go moist. "And they say Elizabeth went up to her room as a princess and came down as a queen, like in a fairy story. We all thought it was very significant, very appropriate that she ascended to the throne *in* Kenya."

Mum pronounces the name of the country with a long, colonial-era *e* — Keen-ya (/ki nja/), as if Britain still stains more than a quarter of the globe pink with its dominion. I, however, pronounce it with a short, post-colonial *e* — Kenya (k nja). It irritates my mother when I say "Kenya" and she corrects me, "Keen-ya," she says. But her insistence on the anachronistic pronunciation of the country only adds to my impression that she is speaking of a make-believe place forever trapped in the celluloid of another time, as if she were a third-person participant in a movie starring herself, a perfect horse and flawless equatorial light. The violence and the injustices that came with colonialism seem — in my mother's version of events — to have happened in some other unwatched movie, to some other unwatched people.

Which in a way, they were.

Sometime in the late 1940s the General Council of the banned Kikuyu Central Association began a campaign of civil disobedience. They were protesting the British takeover of Kenyan land and the colonial labor laws that forced black Kenyans into a feudal system structured to benefit the eighty thousand white settlers. "No," Mum says impatiently. "No, no, no, you've got it all wrong. Eldoret was not taken over from anyone. There hadn't been anyone living on it before the white man came. It was too bleak and windy for the natives. The Nandi lived in the warm forests around the plateau. Plus, they weren't farmers. They were cattle people and they were very independent, very savage, very serious warriors." Mum pauses. "So we all got on rather well together." Then she gives voice to a common settler sentiment. "It was not the Nandi who were the problem, it was the Kikuyu who were so difficult."

Known to themselves as Muingi (the Movement), Muigwithania (the Understanding) or Muma wa Uiguano (the Oath of Unity), the rebellion became known outside Kikuyu circles as the Mau Mau. Possibly the name was an acronym of the Kiswahili phrase "Mzungu Aende Ulya. Mwafrika Apate Uhuru" — "Let the White Man Go Back. Let the African Go Free." Or perhaps it was a mispronunciation of "Uma, Uma" — "Get out, Get out."

Members of the Mau Mau bound themselves together through traditional Kikuyu oath rituals that were rumored to involve animal sacrifice, the ingestion of human and animal blood, cannibalism and bestiality. They used traditional Kikuyu weapons — spears, short swords, rhino hide whips, and broad-bladed machetes — and frequently tortured their victims, disemboweled them and hacked them beyond recognition. In early 1952 the bodies of several Kikuyu policemen loyal to the British were discovered mutilated and bound with wire, floating in rivers near Nairobi. Not long after, settler famers near Mount Kenya found their cattle disemboweled in the fields, the tendons in their legs severed.

"No," Mum says, "we didn't enjoy the Kikuyu. They were very scary and up to all sorts of horrible, funny business. That made us all very anxious even on the plateau. We sent the servants home before dark, locked the house at night and put chicken wire up over the windows. My father went everywhere with his service revolver and my mother kept a Beretta pistol under her pillow."

Still, nothing happened to the Huntingfords or to any of their friends. Life went on in all its gauzy, cinematic glory. Then one day in mid October 1952, a note arrived at the Huntingfords' door carried by one of Babs Owens's syces. The syce was breathless with fright. A Kikuyu insurgent had appeared on the racecourse. "I can't think why Babs had to fetch my father for help," Mum says. "You'd have thought, being Babs, she could have walloped the bloke herself, or bitten his ear off or something, but she didn't. She sent this note to my father and he was a gentleman, so he grabbed his revolver and off he went, across the road."

My grandfather kept his back to the ruins

and made his way cautiously behind the track. In the unfiltered equatorial light, the crumbling buildings from the Italian prisoner-of-war camp set up spooky blue shadows. "The old jail, all abandoned and gloomy," Mum says. Suddenly my grandfather saw the alleged Kikuyu dart briefly into the open then sink into the dimness of one of the dissolving buildings. "My father edged his way up to the building and fired a warning shot into the building. He didn't intend to shoot the chap, obviously, but the bullet ricocheted off the walls and hit him — didn't kill him. Just a wound. But now it was a police matter and my father was carted off to appear in court."

Mum shakes her head. "A few days later and it would have been fine for my father to shoot a Kikuyu because the British had declared a state of emergency by then. But on that afternoon it wasn't okay." A trial was held and my grandfather was sentenced to one day in jail. There was an outcry from the community. "My father was the starter at the races that afternoon," Mum explains. "He couldn't possibly spend the day in jail. He was the only one who knew how to do the starter flags."

After the state of emergency was declared, British soldiers poured into the country and white settlers joined their ranks. By the end of November 1952, eight thousand Kikuyu had been arrested. Far from subduing the tension, attacks against British settlers escalated. Until January 1953, Mau Mau attacks against settlers were isolated and only men were targeted. But on the twenty-fourth of that month, the hacked and tortured bodies of a young British settler family were discovered on their farm — Roger Rucks (aged thirty-seven), his pregnant wife, Esmee (aged thirty-two), and their son, Michael, (aged six). Their Kikuyu cook (tellingly, his name and age were not given in any of the reports) had also been beaten and chopped to death.

Settlers fired their Kikuyu servants, and arrests of suspected Kikuyu insurgents as well as of innocent Kikuyu bystanders intensified. By the end of 1954, British soldiers were holding as many as seventy-seven thousand Kikuyu men, women and children in cramped, unhygienic concentration camps. They forced detainees to work, and if they refused, the prisoners were beaten, sometimes to death. One prisoner, John Maina Kahihu, describes the atmosphere in these camps vividly: "We refused to do this work. We were fighting for our freedom. We were not slaves. . . . There were two hundred guards. One hundred seventy stood around us with machine guns. Thirty guards were inside the trench with us. The white man in charge blew his whistle and the guards started beating us. They beat us from 8 am to 11.30. They were beating us like dogs. I was covered by other bodies — just my arms and legs were exposed. I was very lucky to survive. But the others were still being beaten. There was no escape for them."*

Jittery settlers made plans to leave Kenya, hastily selling their farms and setting sail for Australia or Britain. Forever after they would bore to death anyone who would listen about the perfect equatorial light of East Africa. "When-wes" they were called, as in, "When we were in Kenya. . . ." But everyone understood that the old colonial Kenya was over. No matter how many British soldiers were sent to the colony, no matter how many Kikuyu were shot or arrested, the minority's complacent picnic on the backs of a deeply angry majority was over.

At about this time, Flip Prinsloo returned to the Huntingfords' door and asked to see my grandmother. Once again, my grandmother sat out on the veranda with Flip

*From *Imperial Reckoning: The Untold Story of Britain's Gulag in Kenya* by Caroline Elkins (New York: Henry Holt and Company, 2005).

and poured them both a glass of homemade wine. "Here's to us," she said, raising her glass.

"Ja," Flip agreed. He turned his glass in his hand for some moments before taking a drink. "Well," he said after the sting of the wine had subsided enough to let him speak. "You've lost this war."

"Yes, we already know that," my grandmother said.

They finished their drinks in near silence and then Flip got to his feet. "We're going back to South Africa," he said.

"So I heard," my grandmother said. She lifted the bottle. "Won't you stay and have the other half?"

"Nee dankie." Flip jammed his veldskoen hat back on his head. Then he took a deep breath. "If your daughter wants the horse, I'll take a hundred pounds for it." He stood his ground for a moment as if expecting the money to materialize on the spot.

"I see," my grandmother said.

Flip nodded and in the intervening moments the fragile peace that my grandmother and he had made between the British and the Boers reverted to mutual suspicion. "Good-bye, Mrs. Huntingford," Flip said.

"God speed to you, Mr. Prinsloo," my grandmother replied.

My grandmother watched Flip Prinsloo's retreating back and poured herself a fortifying glass of wine. A hundred pounds was far beyond the Huntingford budget. An advertisement went up on the sports club notice board and another appeared on the notice board at the race grounds. "FOR SALE: Violet." And then it listed all her achievements: "Winner of this, that and the next thing," Mum says. "Everyone knew Violet; she hardly needed to be advertised."

Mum sulked and wouldn't talk to anyone for weeks. "Luckily no one would buy her," Mum says. "She was so difficult. Anyway, lots of people were leaving and everyone was trying to get rid of their animals. No one wanted to take on more responsibility." In the end, Flip Prinsloo couldn't sell Violet and he had to give Mum the mare for nothing. She smiles. "So that was one good thing that came out of the Mau Mau."

Although most of their friends had packed up, my grandparents didn't immediately consider leaving Kenya. "Certainly Australia was out of the question," Mum says. "And I don't suppose my parents felt they had any reason to be in Britain. Dad felt Kenyan. It was his home." So instead of leaving, the Huntingfords bought half a farm on a long, low basin about five miles north of the racetrack. Catherine Angleton, the rich one-legged English widow with whom my grandmother had boarded during the war, bought the other half on the condition that her son Martin could come out to Kenya and live on it.

"Auntie Glug told me Martin was smelly and had a prehensile forehead," I say.

"Did she?" Mum says, frowning.

"Yes," I say.

"I suppose you're going to go putting that into an Awful Book," Mum says.

"Well?" I persist.

"Oh, I suppose," Mum admits reluctantly. "Yes, there was a bit of a problem so none of the girls wanted to go out with him and that led to much more serious problems."

"Like what?" I ask.

Mum gives me a look. "Just more serious problems," she says darkly.

Mum was nearly sixteen by the time the Mau Mau uprising had been quelled in January 1960. Fewer than a hundred Europeans had been killed. Official British sources estimated that British troops and Mau Mau rebels had killed more than eleven thousand black Kenyans, but in a 2007 article in *African Affairs,* the demographer John Blacker estimated the total number of black Kenyan deaths at fifty thousand, half of whom were children under ten. The insurgency had been quashed, but news of atrocities British soldiers and white settlers had committed made headlines in Britain and the British lost their stomach for the colony. "Independence was inevitable," Mum says.

In preparation for self-rule in Kenya, African leaders pressed for the resettlement of those Kikuyu who had been incarcerated in the labor and concentration camps during the Mau Mau. In July 1960, government officials arrived on the Huntingfords' farm and begged my grandparents to take in a Kikuyu family. My grandfather looked out at his little farm, with its freshly planted windbreaks and carefully contoured lands. "I don't see why not," he said.

Duly, the Njoge family set up their homestead upwind of Martin Angleton's little thatched shack. Martin traveled downwind to welcome them to the farm. "And the next thing you know people started teasing my father at the club, asking him if he had put up the banns." Mum blinks at me, as if the astonishment of this moment has not yet worn off. "It turned out that Martin had gone and got himself engaged to Mary Njoge." Mum narrows her eyes. "Well, the wedding went off without a hitch. Everyone brought a fish slice or whatever it was. And that was that — the new Kenya." Mum pauses, "So you can say what you like, but we were all very progressive." She has to search for the other word. "Yes," she says at last, *egalitarian.*

In 1961, the year she turned seventeen, it was decided something should be done with Mum. "My parents wanted me to learn how to be useful and that wasn't going to happen as long as I stayed in Kenya." They sent her to Mrs. Hoster's College for Young Ladies in London and put her up in a women's hostel in Queensgate. "I'll never forget — as soon as you opened the door, there was this awful stench of overcooked cabbage," Mum says. "Then I suppose they got extractor fans and blew it all up into the ozone and now it doesn't smell so bad, but back then the whole of England reeked of boiled cabbage."
Mrs. Hoster's College for Young Ladies was a very reputable establishment opposite the Natural History Museum in South Kensington, "run by a bunch of scary, tweedy lesbians. Although some very noble people went there." She shuts her eyes and counts them off on two fingers. "Prince Philip's assistant went there, passionate about being posh. And the Dalai Lama's sister — she went there too, passionate about the cause."

Every morning, students at Mrs. Hoster's College for Young Ladies were stationed behind Remington typewriters. "About two tons of steel, and they would put on records of military music and we were supposed to type in time to the Coldstream Band. Clickety-clack, clickety-clack." Then Mum gives a rendition of herself typing. "On the other hand — pause, ping — pause, ping — pause, ping. That was my corner." And in the afternoon shorthand practice. "Well, I could never read back what I had written — it just looked like a madwoman's scrawl to me."

Mum sighs. "It took me longer to complete the course than everyone else because I was not passionate about being a secretary. And I had chronic sinus problems." She hesitates and then corrects herself. "Actually, not really. It was London in the sixties. There was so much going on. I didn't have sinus problems at all, I had hangovers."

"You were a hippie?" I ask.

"Hippie?" repeats Mum coldly. "Don't be ridiculous, Bobo. No, these were the years of the Cold War; lots of lovely intrigue and hanky-panky — the Profumo affair, Mandy Rice-Davies, Christine Keeler. We all confidently expected that we were going to get blown to pieces by the Russians at any moment; it was terribly exciting." Mum shakes her head, "And I wasn't going to die learning bloody shorthand, that's for sure."

Catherine Angleton offered to hold a ball so that my mother could come out. "Not out of the closet," Mum says, as if this is what I am about to suggest. "I was supposed to creep out from behind the typewriter to be formally presented to society. But I didn't want to be a debutante. I didn't see the point. Anyway, the sort of Englishmen who went to those balls would have sneered at me because I was a colonial." She sighs. "They'd all have been terribly snobbish and listened like hawks for a slip in my accent; if I made the slightest mistake with my pronunciation, they would have pounced."

Years later, Mum tried to drill proper accents into Vanessa and me. Hours and hours of BBC radio were streamed into our ears in the hope that Received Pronunciation would rub off on us. And she did what she could to bring our voices down an octave or two — our high-pitched Rhodesian accents made us sound like adenoidal chipmunks. Auntie Glug thought we sounded sweet; Mum thought we sounded appalling.

My current accent is, according to Mum, appalling too — a hybrid Southern-African-English-American patois, barely recognizable as the language of Elizabeth II. My sister isn't much better. She came home from the time she spent in London in her late teens and early twenties with what Mum calls "a dreadful cockney twang" to complement her colonial clip. "I can never tell if Vanessa is deliberately trying to wind me up," Mum says, "or if she just does these things because she doesn't care."

When I ask Vanessa which of these it is, she takes a long drag off her cigarette and says, "Both."

In addition to being bombarded by Received Pronunciation, Vanessa and I were instructed in a bewildering list of prohibitions regarding speech and vocabulary. It was vulgar to talk about money, which suited us because we seldom had any worth mentioning. (Money was also supposed to be frivolously frittered — when Mum finally came into a small inheritance upon her mother's death in 1993, she spent it on books, horses, Royal Ascot hats and a protracted visit to London's West End, where she saw every show playing.) It was also vulgar to talk about one's health. "No one *really* wants to know how you are," Mum said, "so just tell everyone you're marvelous." We had to say *napkin* instead of *serviette, loo* instead of *toilet, veranda* instead of *stoep, sofa* instead of *settee,* and *what?* instead of *pardon?* We were told it was rude to ask if someone wanted "*another* drink." You always asked if they wanted "*a* drink" or "the other half."

At school, however, the matrons gave us milk of magnesia for our bowels even when we told them we were "marvelous." The teachers thought *what?* and *loo* were uncouth. They corrected Vanessa and me, and told us to say *pardon?* and *lavatory.* Meanwhile, half the students at our school thought being posh meant excessive primness and drinking their tea with a raised pinkie. The other half didn't care at all about manners and cultivated a deliberate unposhness. I did my best to fit in.

"Well, it's up to you," Mum said. "But don't blame me if you're invited to tea with the Queen, and don't have a clue how to behave."

By December 1963, it was decided that all that could be done for Mum at Mrs. Hoster's College for Young Ladies had been done. "After two whole years, I still couldn't type and I couldn't do shorthand." Her eyes flame. "They tried to tame me and they failed." A week later, Mum left London and landed in perfect, equatorially lit Nairobi. "I had my hair dyed blond and cut shoulder length, very sophisticated," she says. "Those were the days when you dressed to the nines to fly and I wanted to look my best for Kenya." She wore navy blue winklepickers and a pale blue linen suit. "Off the rack but it gave the impression of being very posh — short enough to be intriguing but not so short as to upset the horses." Mum smiles. "And oh, I'll never forget the first breath of Kenyan air when I stepped off that plane — so fresh, so fragrant. And the light was so perfect, such unpolluted clarity." She gives me a look. "Lots of people have tried to write about it, you know, but hardly anyone can capture it. You had to be there. You had to see it for yourself."

What Mum does not say is that by the time she came home from England, Kenya was an independent country. In May 1963, the Kenya African National Union won the country's first general election. As news of the results were released, thousands of Kenyans ran through the rain-drenched streets of Nairobi cheering, "Uhuru! Uhuru!" Jomo Kenyatta, the seventy-three-year-old former secretary of the Kikuyu Central Association, addressed the nation, calling for tribal and racial differences to be buried in favor of national unity. "We are not to look to the past — racial bitterness, the denial of fundamental rights, the suppression of culture," he said. "Let there be forgiveness." On December 12, 1964, the Republic of Kenya was proclaimed, and Mzee Jomo Kenyatta became Kenya's first president.

"Yes, well," Mum says.

PART TWO

O wye en droewe land, alleen
Onder die groot suidesterre. . . .
Jy ken die pyn en eensaam lye
van onbewuste enkelinge,
die verre sterwe op die veld,
die klein begrafenis. . . .

Oh wide and sad land, alone
Under the great southern stars. . . .
You know the pain and lonely suffering
of ignorant individuals,
the remote death in the veld,
the little funeral. . . .

    — DIE DIEPER REG. 'N SPEL VAN DIE OORDEEL
        OOR 'N VOLK, N.P. VAN WYK LOUW

Tim Fuller of No Fixed Abode

Dad. Paris, 1958.

Dad is an upholder of the stiff-upper-lip adage: "If you don't have anything nice to say about somebody, then don't say anything at all." Consequently, he is almost completely silent on the subject of his family. To be fair, his family have been equally silent on their own behalf and conspicuous for their almost total absence from our lives. Although, with our congenitally bad plumbing, land mines on the roads, snakes in the pantry and so on, it's hard to blame Dad's relatives for their lack of interest in coming to visit us.

Occasionally a relentlessly cheerful letter would arrive from England from Dad's younger brother, Uncle Toe. And at Christmas, his wife, Auntie Helen, would sometimes send gifts of deliriously rare contraband (makeup for Vanessa and me, Irish linen tea cloths for Mum). But these infrequent communications seemed only to emphasize the enormous divide between the Fullers (us) who were sweating away in southern Africa and the Fullers (them) who we imagined were pinkly middling it out in Yorkshire or London or Oxford. And once or twice, at Mum's insistence, we drove two hours west from the farm in the Burma Valley to visit the only relative of my father's who had moved to Africa. "Cousin Zoo is blood family," Mum told us firmly, "and blood" — she presented us with a fist — "Blood is blood."

Zoo was terribly English and scrupulously if dutifully hospitable. She treated Vanessa and me as if we were visiting budgerigars that needed to be fed and then put somewhere dark for the night. And although Zoo seemed genuinely fond of Dad, it was chiefly his wasted eligibility that concerned her. "Your father was *terribly* good looking, *terribly* promising," she would tell Vanessa and me. "He was our absolutely favorite cousin." Accordingly, she arranged for my parents to sleep apart while under her roof: Mum in a spare bedroom, Dad locked in the workshop. It was as if Zoo hoped that a single night's separation could erase or undo this inappropriately wild colonial marriage.

Dad had been in Kenya only two weeks when he happened to be at the airport in Nairobi to meet the flight from England. "I suppose I was there to pick up someone, I can't remember who," Dad says. "All I remember is seeing this blonde get off the airplane in a pale blue outfit." It was, of course, Mum, fresh from Mrs. Hoster's College for Young Ladies. "Whew, you can't imagine what your mother looked like, Bobo. Even from a distance, she knocked the wind out of a chap." He leans over now and pats her hand. "Do you come here often or only in the mating season?" he asks. (It's one of Dad's old gags, borrowed from the BBC *Goon Show*, but Mum lights up as if it's the first time she's heard it.)

For her part, Mum was swayed by Dad's baggy, knee-length Bermuda shorts. "Everyone else was in these horrible, tight little schoolboy boxer shorts with the pockets hanging out the bottom," she says. So when Dad asked her to marry him, less than a month after they met, Mum said yes. Dad telegraphed England with the news of his engagement and the answer came back from his father, "Is she black? Stop. Don't do it. Stop." But my parents went ahead with their plans anyway. They were married in Eldoret on July 11, 1964. Photographs of that day are overwhelmingly (indeed solely) lopsided in favor of the bride: my grandfather is caught guffawing over a glass of champagne, my grandmother looks oppressed by the formal arrangement of flowers on her hat, Auntie Glug bursts out of her bridesmaid's dress, Mum's friends look drunk (in an outdoorsy, wholesome *pukka*-pukka sahib way).

No one from Dad's side of the family came to the wedding, and their absence is the beginning edge of everything that followed. Mum is completely flanked but Dad is unsupported and what this will do to him is evident, the way his eyes already register a kind of wary separation from the rest of the world. Even with Mum by his side in each of these wedding photographs — maybe especially with her by his side (she overflowing with serene confidence, he with a monumental hangover) — Dad seems profoundly alone.

Perhaps because of this uneven beginning, we are defined less by my father than by my mother's culture, people and family. Mum is African in her orientation, so we think of ourselves as African. She believes herself to be a million percent Highland Scottish in her blood, so we think of ourselves as springing onto African soil from somewhere wild and English-hating. My siblings and I are more than half English but this is hardly ever acknowledged. Even Hodge's lengthy Anglican heritage (all those Church of England Bishops and vicars) is a footnote after the fact that he signed up to fight in the Second World War as "Scotch."

And although my father is profoundly English, by the time I am old enough to know anything about him, he is already fighting in an African war and his Englishness has been subdued by more than a decade on this uncompromising continent. In this way, the English part of our identity registers as a void, something lacking that manifests in inherited, stereotypical characteristics: an allergy to sentimentality, a casual ease with profanity, a horror of bad manners, a deep mistrust of humorlessness. It is my need to add layers and context to the outline of this sketchy Englishness that persuades me to ask my reticent father about himself: I am searching for the time before he was alone, for the time when he was part of a tribe and a place. I am looking for the person he was before he became the man who would never ask for help, even if not doing so meant our lives.

If Mum's childhood was set in a happily cramped, converted World War II officers' barracks under perfect equatorial light on the wind-blown gold of the Uasin Gishu plateau, the majority of Dad's childhood was set in Hawkley Place, a coldly large Victorian house in Liss, fifty miles south of London. "I spent my whole life outside, watching the haying or trailing around after the cowman from next door," Dad says. He opens his penknife and uses it to scrape out his pipe and absentmindedly checks the blade against his thumb. "So that was good fun," he says.

Dad's parents had spent the first years of their marriage stationed in China. "I think they might have been happy there," Dad says uncertainly. But he can't produce any proof or details because by the time he arrived on the scene, on March 9, 1940, in Northampton Hospital, England, any romance or affection that once may have existed between his parents had long since burned off.

"China," Mum muses. "How wonderful! Where in China?" she asks, but before Dad can answer, Mum's mind leaps to Doris Day. "Shanghai in the 1930s," she says. "What do you think?" And then she starts singing about leaving for Shanghai and being allergic to rice. "Tra la la la la laaaaa!" she finishes when she runs out of words, which is pretty soon.

This is the second day of our South African holiday. Mum, Dad and I are sitting in the garden of a tranquil lodge in the Cederberg Mountains, drinking tea. In the background, Cape turtle doves are calling the day to a mournful close, "Work hard-er, work hard-er." A flock of guinea fowl croon in the field in front of us. White egrets flock across the sky to their roost. The cliffs behind us are struck golden pink by the setting sun. But the rareness of this exceptional peace is made still more singular by the fact that Dad is sitting still and he is speaking.

"Most talk is just noise pollution," he says. At home in Zambia, you can hear him stamping into the kitchen for his tea long before dawn, muttering a greeting to the dogs, lighting his pipe. He is usually out of the camp, pacing the length of the irrigation pipes, checking the height of the river long before the rest of us have managed our first cup of tea.

At lunchtime — when the farm's staff takes an afternoon break and the land itself seems to exhale heat — Dad will retreat from the punishing sun and sit under the Tree of Forgetfulness with his *Farmers Weekly* or catch up with a month-old *London Telegraph* crossword puzzle, but the activity is less restful than it sounds. His pipe is constantly moving from mouth to ashtray, and then (tap-tap-tap) it is emptied, refilled, lit, extinguished, scraped out, refilled yet again and so on. Then at four o'clock, the lengthening shadows seem to act as an irresistible lure. He clamps his pipe between his teeth and strides out of camp, back into his bananas or around the boundary of the farm. In Dad's ordinary day, there is no room for reminiscences.

Dad's mother, Ruth — "Boofy" — was the youngest of six Garrard daughters: Garrard, of the Crown Jewelers, the oldest jewelers in the world, by appointment to HRH, the Prince of Wales. "And being a Garrard, everyone supposed Boofy had inherited a lot of money," Mum says. "Actually, her chief Garrard inheritance was thick ankles." Mum looks complacently at her own slim, tanned legs. "Poor Boofy," she says.

What nobody says, but all of us know, is that Boofy was a catastrophic drunk, a legacy from her spectacularly alcoholic grandmother who died after falling leglessly backward into the fireplace. It would be logical to suppose that this would have put Dad off drinkers for life. On the contrary, nothing short of drinking a bottle of gin before breakfast for a decade at a time will convince Dad that a person has a real problem with alcohol. Moreover, a hangover is almost the only ailment for which he is likely to consider offering a person a consoling aspirin. Heart attacks, diabetes, influenza and migraines he regards as purely psychological. But admit to the effects of a late night and Dad is uncharacteristically caring. "Bad luck," he'll say, doling out a couple of tablets, "it must have been something you ate."

Dad's father, Donald Hamilton Connell-Fuller, was a commodore in the British navy (the position doesn't translate to civilian life, where he was relegated to the rank of captain). To the world Dad's father presented a witty, charming and devastatingly handsome front. But, "No, not tolerant," Mum says. "And he had cold blue eyes like a dead fish." She puts down her teacup for a moment and gives me her best impression of a flayed haddock. "He was very ambitious and he had a very short temper." Donald made captain in 1942, when he was just thirty-three years old, and commodore shortly after that, but he never did make admiral, or even rear admiral, and he was bitter about it. "It didn't help that wives were supposed to be supportive in those days, and poor Boofy would show up at regimental dinners with a flask of gin in her handbag and had to be carried out feet first before the fish course was served," Mum says.

Concerned and preoccupied with their own deep disappointments and thwarted ambitions, the Fullers didn't do much with their two young sons. There were no books at bedtime or visits to the cinema, no evening walks and very few meals together. "Sometimes we would be allowed on the battleships, and that was exciting," Dad says. "And once in a while, my father played golf with Toe and he shot rabbits with me. Plus, there was one summer he took us both on a caravanning holiday in Ireland." Dad pauses. "A lonely beach and it rained every day."

Even from the distance of so many years and with the whole beautiful, fierce continent of Africa between me and the sodden Irish beach, I can feel the gloomy failure of that holiday in the pit of my stomach. "Oh God, that's awful," I say.

"The English after the war," Mum explains. "So unhappy. So gloomy. So much boiled cabbage."

By now in our secluded kloof in the Cederberg, the doves in the tree above our heads are wing clattering into their night's sleep. A single baboon in the cliffs barks a warning and the warm world feels leopard watched. A breeze picks up in the meadow and blows the cereal scents of grass and old heat-struck earth toward us. On an ordinary evening, we would have moved inside — a central African's reflex against malarial mosquitoes — but on this inimitable night, none of us stir, the way no one gets up and leaves between movements at a concert.

"Anyway," Dad says, at last, "there was always Noo. She was very good, very kind." And it does seem telling that the presence of a Norland nurse, Irene Stanland — "Noo" — is felt on the edge of every photograph I have ever seen of Dad's childhood, her off-camera, sterilized hands hovering at the ready to pluck my uncertainly smiling dad and his younger brother back to the nursery, where they were expected to be Seen But Not Heard in the manner of Blackie.

Blackie was Noo's passionately adored cat. Even in the ration years after the war, the cat ate a pound and a half of prime steak a week. When he eventually died of complications from obesity, Noo had a taxidermist in London stuff him in an upright, sitting position. So there he sat on her bedside table, flatteringly slimmer than he had been in life and commendably uncomplaining. "It's just the way it was in those days," Dad says. "You spent your whole life sitting bolt upright and you only spoke when spoken to."

It was the earth — the ground beneath his feet — that was the chief joy of Dad's childhood. Every Christmas, and for several weeks of the summer, Dad and Uncle Toe were shipped off to Douthwaite Estate in the Yorkshire Dales to stay with their grandparents, Admiral Sir Cyril and Lady Edith Fuller. "I can close my eyes," Dad says, "and picture that whole estate perfectly. Five farms all put together, rolling hills. Lovely, deep loam. . . ." Dad rubs his fingers together, as if he can even now feel the peaty softness of that old land, "No, you don't find soil like that every day."

Three miles of driveway led up through pastures in which dairy cows grazed picturesquely. In five-acre coppices pheasants were bred, streams were full of trout and fields were teeming with rabbits and foxes. "We used to sing that hymn at chapel, you know?" Dad takes a breath and begins to sing softly into the supporting warmth of the South African night, "And did those feet in ancient time walk upon England's mountains green?" He shakes his head, smiling, and taps out his pipe in his hand, the burned tobacco making a little black pyramid of ash in his palm.

Dad remembers his grandmother Lady Edith as very elegant and thin. He doesn't remember Admiral Sir Cyril at all and my great-grandfather therefore remains insouciantly handsome in a photograph I found for sale at a retailer of "Fine Historic and Autographed Documents" in Missouri of all unlikely places. On the back of the photograph is a barely grammatical and ambiguous note: "On Saturday His Majesty conferred about fifty two Decorations on Naval and Military Officers, one of the officers, Captain Cyril Fuller, R.N., received three Decorations, the C.M.G., the D.S.O., and the Board of Trade Bronze Medal for Saving Life at Sea. Caption Fuller has rendered conspicuous service in Nigeria, and the Board of Trade conferred their medal on him in recognition of this gallantry when a whaler capsized in the Njong River. On that occasion he endeavored to rescue the crew, and while trying to right the boat was twice pulled away by the struggling natives. He succeeded however in saving a number of lives."

I wonder aloud what the natives might have been struggling to do.

Dad sucks on his pipe in silence for a while. "Did they have whalers on Nigerian rivers?" he asks at last. "I suppose they must have." He looks mildly shocked. "Imagine that," he says.

When he was thirteen, Dad's parents got a divorce — "a terrible, terrible thing in those days" — and Hawkley Place was sold. "After that," Dad says, "we were a bit homeless during the holidays." Donald went to sea and stayed there more or less permanently. Boofy bought a country cottage in Sussex ("Very good address, rather shabby house," Mum adds), just large enough for herself and Noo. Home, such as it was, evaporated and in its place came broken holidays, the uncertainty of half-unpacked suitcases, the panic of unbelonging.

Uncle Toe and Dad were shipped off to

various kind and/or dutiful relatives. "I remember one lot, the Shaws," Dad says. "They were a fun, sporting family. They had about four hundred dogs, a Shetland pony in the kitchen and there was always someone hobbling about with a broken arm or a broken leg. One year, Cousin Anti went off to the Himalayas for about six months to find the abominable snowman. I was very impressed."

Five years later Dad reacted to his shape-shifting childhood, breaking generations of tradition. "Everyone expected I'd go into the navy when I got out of school, but I wasn't interested. I always said that I wouldn't mind going to fight if there was a war on, but I wasn't going to play toy soldiers if there wasn't." Moreover, the sea baffled Dad and left him mostly unmoved. "You can't dig a spade in it." Instead, Dad went to agricultural college and before his last term was up, he had applied to emigrate to Canada. "I always had this idea that I wanted to see how the other half lived. And I wanted to go somewhere that still had wild land. Not quite the abominable snowman, but adventure of some sort, that's what I was after."

Dad hired on as a field hand in Ontario. "The McKinneys," he says. "Lovely people, but teetotalers." It was twenty miles away by bike to the nearest pub. "All right in the summer, but I knew I'd freeze to death in the winter." So at the end of the haying season, Dad answered an advertisement to grow tomatoes in the West Indies, bought himself a safari suit at a department store in Toronto and headed south.

A little under a year after Dad got to Montserrat the tomato operation shut down. "Massive factory, not enough tomatoes," he said. For a few months, he kicked about the Caribbean Beach Club — "sleeping under a palm tree, deep-sea fishing, sailing, tennis. It was pretty alcoholic" — until he washed up on a nearby island working at a beach hotel. "My boss was queer as a coot, so I had to spend my whole life walking backward," Dad says. "Then the finale was when my bar bill exceeded my salary by about ten quid a month." Dad was fired.

Next, he was interviewed for a post as the aide-de-camp to the governor-general of Barbados. "My duties were pretty simple. In the morning I had to take Lady Stow's Pekinese for their daily walk. In the evening I had to drink rum punches and play poker dice with the governor." But this more or less extended cocktail hour came to an abrupt end when Sir John received instructions from the Home Office: in preparation for independence, Barbadians were to be employed wherever possible. No one could argue that a Bajan couldn't walk a Pekinese or drink rum punches as well as an Englishman. Dad found himself out of work again.

"Just about that time, someone mentioned a job in East Africa growing trees," he says. "And that sounded all right to me." Accordingly, Dad arrived in Kenya one afternoon in late November 1963, and the next morning he presented himself to Robert Stocker, of the Wattle Company, for a job interview.

"Do you play rugby?" Robert asked.

Dad peered over the desk. Stocker was second-row forward material, his bulging thighs barely fit under his desk. "Yes," Dad said.

Robert looked up, "Position?" he asked.

"Winger," Dad said.

"Good." Robert made a note in Dad's file. "You've got a job."

Dad was paid almost nothing for doing very little. On Wednesday afternoons, he was expected to show up for rugby practice at the Eldoret Sports Club and on Saturdays he was expected for matches. For the rest of the week, he was given a clapped out Land Rover to drive around three or four thousand acres on the plateau. His job was to measure the girth of wattle trees and keep an eye on a few hundred head of cattle. "Sometimes on my rounds I'd see a Ugandan kob or the odd leopard," Dad says. "And then the whole world would stop. I'd switch off the Land Rover, light my pipe and just watch the animals for an hour or two. I'd completely lose track of time, you know — it was absolutely marvelous."

People often ask why my parents haven't left Africa. Simply put, they have been possessed by this land. Land is Mum's love affair and it is Dad's religion. When he walks from the camp under the Tree of Forgetfulness to the river and back again, he is pacing a lifelong, sacred commitment to all soil learned in childhood. "Bring me my Bow of burning gold," Dad is singing again. Now he pauses and turns to Mum. "How does that hymn go, Tub?"

"Bring me my Arrows of desire," Mum sings. "Bring me my Spear: O clouds unfold!"

"That's right," Dad says.

"Bring me my Chariot of fire!" they sing together.

Both my parents want to be buried on their farm in Zambia when the time comes. Accordingly, Dad has picked a baobab tree above the fish ponds for the site of his grave.

"Just wrap me in a bit of sorry cloth and put me deep enough in the ground that Mum's bloody dogs don't dig me up," he says.

Mum has picked a tree within shouting distance of Dad's. "On the other hand," she says, "I expect a big, elaborate funeral. Sing 'The Hallelujah Chorus,' wear large expensive hats and fling yourself into the grave after me."

NICOLA FULLER AND THE PERFECT HOUSE

Mum and Dad with dogs at Lavender's Corner. Kenya, circa 1965.

Nakuru, the Masai call it, "place of dust," and I imagined the air gritty and restless, deviled with pillars of torn plastic. But when I visit in November 2004, it is the beginning of the short rainy season and stone-colored clouds are hanging over the Great Rift Valley. The damp earth is unmoving beneath a greening-blond savannah, and Lake Nakuru is pink with the ebb and flow of thousands of flamingos. Above the town, the Menengai Crater seems placidly mossy, not at all the demon-dancing Kirima Kia Ngoma of legend. Nakuru, it appears to me, is less a place of red dust than a place of mauve quenching.

I search through all the colors of Nakuru and I find peripheral signs that British settlers were here — the sturdy War Memorial Hospital, a faded mock-Tudor pub, storm drains engineered as if by Roman invaders — but I do not find Lavender's Corner. For this reason, the place stays in my memory as Mum has described it: "A lovely bungalow with a wood shingle roof, an enormous pepper tree at the bottom of the garden and lots of paddocks for the horses."

And in the same way that Lavender's Corner stays in my imagination, perfect and somehow innocent, so does the version of my mother that lived in that miraculous house. She is twenty years old, and her beauty is classical and untested by time and the elements. And in this part of her story, she does not work, in the ordinary sense of the word. And she has not yet known grief, beyond the normal, relatively mild tragedies of a typical colonial childhood. In many ways, I barely recognize this person. She is someone else's mother. She is not the broken, splendid, fierce mother I have.

My parents moved into Lavender's Corner shortly after their wedding. They brought Mum's beloved Violet; a cat named Felix; a German Shepherd named Suzy ("one of the nicest dogs we ever had," Dad says) and a few polo ponies ("Horrible, abused, rescued things that no one else would ride," Mum says). There were also several suitcases of high-heeled fashion boots and winklepickers ("completely impractical, and they've given me bunions now, look!"); trunks of Irish linen; cases of Egyptian cotton; rolls of canvas; pots of paint; crates of china; a set of hunting prints; a few bits of silver; a bronze cast of the Duke of Wellington riding his favorite horse; and a set of Le Creuset pots and saucepans.

"Imagine," Mum says, "those Le Creuset pots have survived all these years. Even now, visitors see them in my kitchen as they come down the stairs in the garden and they say, 'Oh, your pots, how orange and picturesque! I must take a photograph!'" What those visitors to the Tree of Forgetfulness can't know is that they are not only photographing the Le Creuset pots but also the shadow of everything that has not made it this far. Each time Mum set sail or moved to another farm or gave up a country, she had

188

to assess what would fit into a few boxes, what could squeeze into the back of a Land Rover, what could make it across the borders of an unpredictable African country. Considering that Mum has always moved with a full complement of animals and a sizable library, precious few other acquisitions have survived the shift from one place to the next. "Lost, stolen, broken, died, left behind," she says.

After returning from Mrs. Hoster's College in England, Mum had been hired as a secretary at a law firm in Eldoret. "Doris Elwell, the other secretary, could type so fast sparks flew from her machine," Mum says. "Well, she'd been a typist for the Nuremberg Trials, so she had an unfair advantage. And then there was me: plink-plink-pause, plink-plink-pause. After every few lines — scrunch, scrunch, scrunch — I had to rewind the paper and pour gallons of Wite-Out on all my mistakes. It was a tremendous relief to everyone at Shaw and Caruthers when I got engaged to Tim because in those days, you weren't expected to carry on working after you got married."

Settled at Lavender's Corner — newly wed and cheerfully unemployed — Mum decided to focus on her art. She set up her easel on the veranda and began to paint. "What I saw in front of me," Mum says, "the Rift Valley in every mood. You could do a different painting every single day of exactly the same view. The light, of course, changed all the time. And the savannah, you know, it's not just a big blond blob." And when she ran out of muse, she saddled up Violet and took Suzy for long, meandering rides. "The land wasn't so chopped up by roads and fences in those days and you could go for miles."

Meanwhile, Dad landed a lucrative position with a German veterinary-supply company. "Four hundred people applied for that job," Mum says, "but Tim got it because he swotted up in *Black's Veterinary Dictionary* — 'Penicillin was discovered in 1928 by Alexander Fleming' — that sort of thing. But what really impressed the Germans was Tim's extreme Britishness. The Germans were thrilled. Until they hired him, they hadn't been able to operate competitively in a former British colony for zee obvious reasons. Isn't that right, Tim?"

"What?" Dad says.

"ZEE GERMANS!" Mum shouts. "UNABLE TO OPERATE IN EAST AFRICA BECAUSE OF ZEE WAR."

On Monday mornings, Dad left Mum on the

veranda. "She was always surrounded by her animals, reeking of paints and turpentine," he says, and drove for days, all over Uganda, Tanzania and Kenya, selling supplies to remote large-animal veterinarians. "You could go for miles without seeing much sign of human life. Maybe the odd Masai herdsman or a couple of Samburu warriors waiting in the shadow of an acacia. If you saw another car, you got so excited you stopped and introduced yourself." But Dad found comfort in the emptiness: the lonely ribs of a long, gravel road; a makeshift bed under wild stars in an insect-sung night. "Once you've had a taste of that," Dad says, "you can't go back to the madding crowd."

On Friday evenings, Dad returned to Lavender's Corner. For the occasion, Mum got out of her artist's smock and put on something respectable. "Pedal pushers and a nice linen shirt," Mum says. Then Dad smoked his pipe at the kitchen table and listened to Mum chatter on about her week, while she made a casserole or a curry in the Le Creuset pots. They ate dinner late, with a couple of bottles of cold beer, and watched the moon make its slow traverse across the Rift Valley.

On the weekends, Mum and Dad turned to more patrician pursuits. Dad played polo. Mum show-jumped. They both hunted. "If you could call it hunting," Mum says. "It was more like cross-country of the worst nature." The hunts took place in Molo. At more than eight thousand feet, Molo was one of the coldest communities in the country. Some distance off the main Nairobi road, pressed up against the Mau Forest, the settlers were isolated, uninhibited and uncensored.

"Happy Valley wastrels," I say.

Mum shakes her head. "No," she says. "No, no, no. The Happy Valley wastrels were gone by then. Well, maybe there was the odd survivor limping about. But no, the Molo people just got up to a little bit of common-or-garden hanky-panky. That's all."

The hunts were organized by an English horse vet named Charlie Thompson, who thoroughly approved of all sorts of blood sports: dog fighting, cock fighting, wife swapping. He had an eagle nose, tiny dark eyes, smoked a pipe and walked as if his hips had been locked into their joints. He had lost his riding muscles in some bizarre accident years earlier, about which no one would speak. "The mind boggles," Mum says, but that didn't stop him from riding his stallion, Amos, every chance he got. "Oh, that horse was a magnificent animal, wasn't he, Tim?"

"Oh yes," Dad says. "Yes, that was a very nice horse, a black Thoroughbred with a bit of warm blood in him."

While I am sitting there in astonishment that my parents can remember the name, breeding and color of this long-ago stallion, Mum resumes, "Charlie just strapped himself into the saddle, a classic English seat, and off he'd go. He rode like mad! He had proper hounds too, but instead of foxes, we went after reedbuck."

Hunts would traditionally begin with one of Charlie's famous dinners: piles of mashed potatoes, a leg of some recently slain game animal, beans boiled to death, gallons of bad wine. He lived in a dark cedarwood house furnished with worn leather chairs and moth-eaten animal-skin rugs. On the walls, there were the usual collection of mangy mounted heads and tarnished Indian sabers. "About a thousand bad-tempered dogs were draped everywhere, glaring at you as you ate," Dad says. And there was a parrot. "You would ask for the gravy and the parrot would shout, 'And you can fuck off too!'" Dinner usually ended with port in front of the fire. The generator was switched off at about midnight, and the guests faltered to bed with candles. "And then the corridor creeping started," Dad says. "Mum and I kept our door locked."

"Yes, I'm afraid so," Mum says. "Those

people had to leave their children in a pram at the bottom of the garden until it was time to send them to boarding school because they all looked like the neighbor."

In the morning, everyone gathered out in the yard for the hunt, the hounds thrashing and whining and twining themselves around the horses' legs. "You had to be careful if you had a mare like Violet because Amos was terribly excitable," Mum says. "If you weren't paying attention, the next thing you knew you had Charlie and Amos sidling up, everything sticking out. . . ." A stirrup cup was brought out to the riders. "Usually dry sherry," Mum says, "of which you needed a big strong dollop because it could be awfully cold and the hunt was always bloody dangerous."

Then the horses lined up to leap out of the wooden enclosure. "It was before anyone had taught their horses to jump barbed wire, so there was no other way around," Mum says. "We'd all scramble over these impossibly high livestock pens and then off we'd go through the mist, along the edge of the forest, the hounds baying and the reedbuck springing out ahead of us, usually getting away, thank God." Mum sighs. "Violet just loved it. She would gallop like the wind —

such a big heart, such lungs, the altitude didn't bother her at all. We were always streaks ahead of everyone else."

"Even Amos and Charlie?" I ask.

"*Especially* Amos and Charlie," Mum says.

Then, in early August 1965, at a Charlie Thompson hunt, for the first time in her life, something happened to Mum's nerve. "We were supposed to leap out of this hideous kraal as usual, and I'd done it heaps of times before. But on this day suddenly my heart just wasn't in it. I suppose Violet felt me hesitate because she faltered and I tumbled off." In the end, Dad had to ride Violet over the kraal and Mum walked around. She finished the rest of the ride, but she was uncharacteristically shaken by her fall.

Back at Lavender's Corner, Mum just felt like lying in bed all day. "Of course Suzy would get fed up and make me take her for walks, but exercise made me feel queasy," she says. "The smell of paint made me dizzy. Food turned my stomach. So off I went to the doctor and I explained that I had taken this spill at one of Charlie Thompson's hunts and that I still wasn't feeling right. And he did a couple of tests and told me I was pregnant. I was very indignant. I said, 'No, of course I'm not. You don't get pregnant from falling off a horse. Everyone knows that.'"

However, by early September, the evidence of an impending baby was undeniable. Mum surrendered to her condition and began reading Shakespeare to her womb. "All the studies in those weird, gawd-help-you parenting books said reading aloud to your fetus produced serene, intelligent babies," Mum says.

"But Shakespeare?" I ask.

Mum blinks defensively. "Well, a person might as well start with Shakespeare and work her way through the rest of literature from there." So by the time of her birth, on the evening of March 9, 1966, at Nakuru's War Memorial Hospital, Vanessa Margaret Fuller had been exposed to *King Lear, Macbeth, Hamlet,* most of *Coriolanus,* several sonnets and all the major comedies. She was blond, blue eyed and preternaturally calm. Mum shrugs. "How was I to know it was going to put her off reading for the rest of her life?"

Mum brought her new baby back to Lavender's Corner and her perfectly-lit, cinematic life continued on schedule. Vanessa slept through the night from about the day she was born. "She hardly ever fussed. I just fed her occasionally and put her in a pram at the bottom of the garden," Mum says.

"Because she looked like the neighbor?" I ask.

Mum gives me a look. "No, Bobo, Vanessa did not look the least bit like the neighbor, more is the pity for your Awful Books." There's a pause while Mum allows me to feel deeply ashamed of my cast aspersions. "No," she continues. "I put her at the bottom of the garden so that I could get on with my painting." My mother sighs. "Well, I thought she'd be all right because she was a very placid child and she had Suzy to look after her. Suzy was very protective. God help anyone who got anywhere near Vanessa's pram."

And so one sunny, bright morning in late June, Mum put Vanessa under the pepper tree, as usual, and returned to the veranda to paint. Vanessa was still too young to sit up or do much of anything except continue to process the indigestible amount of Shakepeare that had been read to her as a fetus. Meanwhile, the dry season had started, and the light had taken on a quality of bushfires and dust. "Oh, the colors that day. I'll never forget. It was all ocher with shades of purple," Mum says. "You know? One gets absorbed by the world."

An hour or so later, out of the corner of her

eye, Mum became aware of Suzy racing back and forth from the bottom of the garden to the veranda, trying to get her attention. She dropped her paintbrush and ran out onto the lawn.

"Vanessa was gone," Mum says. "I looked around wildly. But I couldn't see her and I couldn't hear her. And then finally I noticed the pram, twenty feet off. Somehow the brake had come undone, and it had rolled away and tipped up. Vanessa was all bundled in the hood, covered in blankets. She was absolutely crimson in the hot sun." Mum shakes her head. "I got such a fright," she says. "That was it. I never painted again."

Before the dry season had ended, a further accumulation of mishaps and tragedies bumped up against history and by the beginning of the next short rains, my mother was in a world she couldn't recognize. First, one of Dad's polo ponies chased Violet through a barbed wire fence. "I found her standing in the paddock, her belly ripped open, her neck bleeding, her legs in ribbons," Mum says. Mum sent an urgent note to Charlie Thomson up in Molo and meantime she tried smearing May & Baker powders and liquid paraffin on the wounds. Violet trembled. Blood gushed down Mum's arms.

Charlie arrived the next day. He shook his head. "Better to destroy her," he said. "It really would be kindest." But looking at Mum's face, he surrendered and gave Violet something for the pain and something else to limit the spread of infection. "It would really be kindest . . ." he started to say again, but Mum shook her head. Charlie left. For another day and night, Mum stayed with Violet. Every six or eight hours, the alarmed ayah brought Vanessa to the paddock. Mum fed the baby distractedly, never taking her eyes off the mare.

Dad came home on Friday afternoon to find both Mum and Violet half mad with exhaustion. Mum trying to hold the horse upright. Violet trying to die. "If I let go of her, she'll give up," Mum said.

Dad stroked the mare's neck. "Yes," he said, "she will." He waited with Mum an hour or so. Then he said, "All right, Tub."

"I know," Mum said. She dropped the halter rope. The mare sighed, and then slowly lay down, first buckling her knees and then with an enormous effort collapsing her haunches. Mum pulled off her jersey and draped it over the horse's shoulders. "Good-bye, Violet," she said, tears running down her nose and onto the horse's neck. Dad took Mum back to the house and sat her down at the kitchen table with a glass of brandy. He shut every door between Mum and the outside world. Then he went back down to the paddock, scraped as large a hole as he could into the ground and shot Violet.

Mum went to bed for a week, and then another week. When she was tempted to stay in bed for a third week, Granny came down from Eldoret. She sat at the end of Mum's bed with Vanessa on her lap. Mum fed the baby and drank the cups of tea that Granny brought her. She stroked Suzy's ears and let the cat sleep on her pillow, but she couldn't stop crying and she wouldn't go outside. "What's the point?" she kept asking.

What Mum meant was that she'd lost the medium through which she understood her world. She had lost her compass, her frame of reference. "I could look between Violet's ears, and I would know exactly where we were headed," she says. At last, genuinely concerned by the unseemly depth of Mum's grief, my grandmother took her to the doctor, thinking that they all might benefit from a dose of tranquilizers. The doctor did a few tests and then he came back into the office. "This is rather soon," he said.

Both Mum and Granny looked up. The doctor frowned at Mum, so pale and so thin. Then he looked at Vanessa, barely old enough to sit up on her own. "You should pace yourself a little better, Mrs. Fuller," he said.

Mum was pregnant again.

With another baby on the way, Dad considered that two and a half years of driving the length and breadth of East Africa was enough. He wanted a farm, land on which to root his growing family. He pictured an East African version of Douthwaite: dairy cattle, a few good horses, year-round streams, rolling hills. He put money down on a place up in the highlands that fit that description, but before the deal could close, the land officer intervened. "He took me out for a cup of coffee," Dad says, "and told me that the farm I was about to purchase was up for grabs." Dad understood. "The new government had it slated for shambas. If I'd bought it, we would have been thrown off within a year and we would have lost all our investments."

Then my grandparents sold the farm in Eldoret to a dozen small-scale farmers. ("The farmers came to the house with their money tucked around their bodies, in the folds of all their clothes, nothing bigger than a shilling coin," Mum says.) For a few months, my grandparents lived in Nairobi, but eventually they set sail for England for the last time, settling in a semi-detached laborer's cottage near Pangbourne with several crates of books; a smoke-ruined portrait of an ancestral Huntingford bride; carpets worn with the nesting of so many dogs; and a sofa that exhaled a cloud of red Eldoret dust when it was disturbed.

Although they lived in England and then Scotland for the rest of their lives, my grandparents' habits remained Kenyan settler — they grew most of their own vegetables in the garden, my grandfather cultivated and cured his own tobacco, they cooked their meals on a wood stove, they took a quinine pill every night and drank a stiff gin and French at eleven in the morning (after which my grandmother was inclined to walk in circles and blame a congenitally shortened left leg).

"When my mother and father left Kenya that was the end of an era for us," Mum says. "Glug was already in England at university, so we had no other family, and all our friends were leaving. Kenya lost its heart for us. So we looked around. Where else could we move? I knew I couldn't follow my parents to England. My mother was heartbroken, but I knew I wanted to stay in Africa."

What Mum doesn't say, but what she means is that she wanted to stay in White-ruled Africa. In some ways, she doesn't need to say it. Most white Africans either left the continent or receded farther and farther south as African countries in the north gained their independence. The other thing Mum cannot bring herself to say — at least not in so many words — is that her determination to stay in White-ruled Africa was the costliest decision of her life. The worst kind of costly; life and death kind of costly.

The South African garden gathers itself for evening around us. Guinea fowls stop their crooning and roost in the trees by the stables. The sounds of crackling day insects are gradually replaced by the sounds of night: frogs bellowing from the creek, cicadas shrilling from the trees. The colors on the walls of the mountains behind us turn from pink to slate.

"Look," Mum says. "That sun is very nearly down."

"So it is," Dad says.

There's a pause and then Mum flings her

arms in the air, "Drought! Nicola Fuller of Central Africa is experiencing severe drought!"

Dad laughs. "Waiter!" he shouts. "Barman!"

"Help!" shrieks Mum. "Emergency!"

Nicola Fuller in Rhodesia: Round One

Mum with Van. 1966.

Dad with Van. 1966.

The last day of our South African holiday dawns stifling hot. During the night a wind from the northern desert has blown the last of the moderate temperatures south. We're all suffering from slight headaches — "self-inflicted," Mum says — so we sit on the veranda after breakfast drinking tea, too lethargic to bother with our usual morning walk. Dad is smoking his pipe. Mum has a pair of binoculars resting on her lap in case she sees a bird and then the glasses flash to her eyes. "Look at that sweet little thing with a stripy head," she says. She consults her bird book. "It's a Cape bunting, I think. Oh dear, they say in here it's a *very* common resident." She glares at the disappointingly common bird. "We don't get them in Zambia. Do we, Tim?"

"Say again?" Dad says.

"CAPE BUNTING!" Mum shouts. "NOT ONE OF OURS."

The words that changed my parents' lives were few enough and small enough to fit comfortably onto a postage stamp: "Wanted: Manager for ten thousand hectares in Africa." The advertisement, tucked into the classifieds at the back of the Kenyan *Farmers Weekly* didn't name the country in Africa on which these ten thousand hectares existed. It didn't need to. "There was only one country on the continent whose name could not be mentioned," Mum says. "Rhodesia."

At exactly eleven in the morning, Greenwich Mean Time, on November 11, 1965, the Rhodesian government, led by Prime Minister Ian Smith, had rendered their country unmentionable by presenting a Unilateral Declaration of Independence (UDI) to British Prime Minister Harold Wilson. The telegram announcing UDI was timed to arrive at Number 10 Downing Street precisely as Britain began its traditional two-minute silence to mark the end of the First World War. UDI expressly flew in the face of Britain's assertion that there should be no independence before majority rule (NIB-MAR).

The next day, on November 12, 1965, the United Nations Security Council adopted Resolution 216 condemning UDI as an illegal construct of "a racist minority." On the same day, the front page of the *Rhodesian Herald* announced, UDI RHODESIA GOES IT ALONE. Above that headline, in smaller letters, was the news that state censorship had been imposed. On that day, for the first time in its history, blank columns of white space appeared in the newspaper. In the minds of the Rhodesian government, the country was now entirely independent of Britain and it was — and would remain — governed by the white minority.

The "ten thousand hectares in Africa" turned out to belong to John Lytton-Brown, a Kenyan settler. "We didn't know him," Mum says. "He wasn't really one of our set." Not a *pukka*-pukka sahib, in other words.

Dad applied for the job and in January 1967 he set sail from Mombasa to Cape Town en route to Rhodesia. He took with him a change of clothes, a sleeping bag and his *Black's Veterinary Dictionary*. Mum stayed behind to pack up Lavender's Corner. "I didn't hear much from Tim once he got to Rhodesia because of UDI," Mum says. "No telegrams, no phone calls. Letters had to go via Malawi, postmarked Blantyre."

My father's first letter from Rhodesia was cryptic. "Dear Tub," he wrote,

I've settled down alright at Berry's Post. We're not far from the Hunyani River. It's a bit off the beaten path. There's 400 acres of cotton, 200 acres of maize, 200 acres of sunflowers. Also 400 head of cattle. There's rather a dry spell here so the government is practically giving livestock away to anyone with a bit of grazing. It's a bore that we can't all be together. Soon enough, though. I do miss you.

Lots of love,

Tim.

A month later, Mum gave away what she could not carry and boarded a ship in Mombasa with Vanessa, Felix the cat, and Suzy the dog. She took her favorite books, the

Duke of Wellington bronze cast, a couple of the hunting prints, a few linens, and the orange Le Creuset pots. "You could feel Rhodesia long before you got there," Mum says. "You could sense this outlaw nation, this rebel state." And I can tell she likes those words — *outlaw, rebel* — and how they fit in with the idea she has of herself. "British warships patrolled the Mozambique coast to prevent anything getting into Rhodesia via Beira. South African and Rhodesian passengers weren't allowed off the ship. I thought it was very exciting."

But Mum was quickly disillusioned. On the train north from Cape Town to Bulawayo, she watched in horror as the landscape turned drier and harsher and flatter. When Dad had written that "there's rather a dry spell here," it was a colossal understatement. In fact, the country was in the throes of one of the worst droughts on record. In Matabeleland, cattle had begun dying of thirst before Christmas. By January 1967, the late-planted cotton had grown only six inches and defeated farmers had begun to plow it under.

Up in the high veldt it was just as dry. Cultivated crops wilted blue in the fields, wild trees on the kopjes failed to leaf out and thirsty snakes swarmed to Berry's Post to drink the dog's water. "The farmhouse was a funny Spanish style with these big French doors," Mum says. "My first morning there, I found Vanessa looking through the glass eye to eye at a cobra bellied up to her on the other side of the door, tongue flickering. I was so terrified, I hired Tabatha the next day to follow Vanessa around everywhere." Mum, appalled by the hostility of the land, its dusty loneliness, the unrelentingly dry wind, couldn't envision an occasion for her winklepickers.

Within weeks of arriving, Suzy died of tick fever and then Felix was murdered. "We think by the workers," Mum says. "There was a nasty undercurrent in that part of the country. They resented UDI and they didn't like whites. I suppose that's why they killed our cat."

And then, their second month on the farm, my parents woke up in the middle of the night, shocked conscious by a sensation of being watched. "There, standing at the bottom of the bed was the manager who had worked on the farm before us." Mum's eyes go pale. "Well, his ghost anyway. He had shot himself six months earlier, so he wasn't really there." Even on this very warm South African morning, Mum rubs her arms as if cold. "Look." Mum presents me with the evidence of gooseflesh on her skin. "To this day, I get chills talking about it. I'll never, ever forget looking at someone who was not really there, but he *was* there. It wasn't a bad dream, it wasn't a hallucination, it was real." Mum's chin goes up. "Especially being Scottish from the Isle of Skye, I *know* there are ghosts and fairies in our midst." Mum lowers her brow and clarifies, "Proper fairies, not gays and stuff like that." She takes a sip of her tea and then scans the garden with her binoculars to see if any acceptably uncommon birds have shown up. "No," she says at last, "the ex-manager had come to warn us that Lytton-Brown was a crook. He hadn't paid the ex-manager and he wasn't planning to pay us. He was going to wait until it was harvest time and then fire us and take all the profits. Wasn't he, Tim?"

Dad grunts. "Say again."

"FIRE US AND TAKE ALL THE PROFITS!" Mum repeats.

By harvest time, Mum was eight months pregnant. As predicted by the ex-manager's ghost, Lytton-Brown fired my parents as soon as the crop was in and refused to pay them for their season's work. "It was a terrible blow because we had worked so hard and had produced such good yields in spite of the bad rains," Mum says. Dad began legal proceedings, but in the meantime, my parents were homeless and almost penniless. They lived out of their car, "a dubious 1950 Chevy, straight-six engine that would pass anything but a petrol station."

Winter came early and hard. "Pawpaw trees turned black and fell over," Dad says. "The low veldt was scorched with frost. People's boreholes froze solid. I don't know how many farmers went broke, but you could see them on the streets of Salisbury on the bones of their asses." Dad got a job as a bouncer at Salisbury's only nightclub, La Boheme.

"A very sleazy joint," Mum says. "Zilla the Snake Charmer, that sort of thing."

I stare at my father. "Zilla the Snake Charmer?" I say.

Dad blushes and tampers with his pipe, tapping ash out of the bowl and refilling it with tobacco.

"No, Bobo, those were desperate, desperate times, and they called for desperate, desperate measures," Mum says. "It wasn't an easy job — you can just imagine the customers all having a good time, armed to the teeth. And you know what Rhodesians are — they can't see a snake without wanting to blow its head off."

■ ■ ■ ■

My parents' second child, Adrian Connell Fuller, was born on a bitterly cold day in early winter at the Lady Chancellor Maternity Home in Salisbury. "It was a very difficult, very lonely labor," Mum says. "Terribly cruel treatment. All the nurses and doctors were attending other people. They just left me to get on with it. I suppose they knew I was the homeless, penniless wife of the bouncer at La Boheme, so they didn't care about me." But then the child was born, a blond, blue-eyed son, and Mum was overwhelmed with joy. "The happiest day of my life," she has told me, "was the day I held that little baby in my arms for the first time."

When Adrian was a few weeks old, Dad found work building a smelting plant on a nickel mine near Shamva, fifty miles northeast of Salisbury. Dad had never built anything bigger than a chicken coop in his life, "but the money was okay, so I talked my way into it," Dad says. "I had to do something. Four of us couldn't live off the wages of a bouncer." Dad worked all the hours he could get, leaving Mum before dawn and returning after dark.

Mike Dawson, a farmer near Shamva, let my parents live rent free in a cottage on his farm until they could get their feet under them. "You will never, ever forget the kindness of strangers," Mum says, pushing a work-blunted forefinger into the palm of her hand for emphasis, "Such selflessness, such generosity." Mike's wife, Cherry Dawson, was a depressed Australian. "I think she tried to be kind, but we were all struggling. We all had problems. She wasn't from Africa so she didn't have that open-door policy that we all grew up with. We were an added burden for her." Moreover, Adrian's system seemed shocked by the very bitter winter.

The pattern looked like this: Adrian woke up with a frighteningly high temperature and Mum gave him paracetamol syrup. Then because Mum didn't have a car or a telephone, she ran from the cottage over to the main house with Adrian in her arms, trailing Vanessa. She begged Cherry for a lift to the clinic, fifteen miles away in Bindura. "I could tell Cherry resented the intrusion, let alone the cost of the petrol ferrying me back and forth, which I could never afford to repay." By the time Adrian got to the clinic, his fever was back down because of the paracetamol and Mum was told to take him home.

A day or two passed. Mum put blankets on the cottage's dry lawn and prayed that fresh

air and the weak winter sun would somehow penetrate her child's body and boost his
strength. Then the next morning, Adrian
would again throw a frighteningly high temperature, and again Mum trickled paracete-
mol down his throat and ran to the main
house. "It was obvious they were all thinking I was just a neurotic new mother. But I
wasn't. It was such a bad winter, we were so
hard up and Adrian just kept getting sicker
and sicker." So then Mum wrapped Adrian
in wool blankets and kept him inside. And
for a day or two, this appeared to be the
magical formula to keeping her son well.

Until it wasn't.

Then Mum hoped that warmer weather, or
rain, would change the atmosphere, settle
the dust. And like women everywhere and
for all time, she stared at the sky and begged
the universe to do something to heal her
child. And in due course, the very cold season gave way to a warm, dry September.
After that, October came, hot and humid,
but still it did not rain and still Adrian did
not thrive.

By the third week in October, clouds had
been banking against the high veldt violent
with thunder for a month, but when the rain
fell, it hung like a half curtain in the sky,

not touching the earth. And one morning in that third week, not unusually, Adrian woke with a fever and he was crying, a constant, monotonous cry as if he no longer had the energy to express the precise nature of his illness. Mum gave him paracetamol and tried to nurse him, but Adrian wouldn't eat and his fever stayed high even after a second dose of medicine. Once again, Mum wrapped him in a blanket and ran to the main house to beg a lift from Cherry. On the way to the clinic, Mum put her lips against the soft fluff of hair on Adrian's hot skull and silently she implored him, "Please don't give up. Don't give up. It'll get better, you'll see." And she closed her eyes and did her best to picture Adrian at twelve, at eighteen, at thirty, as if her sheer will could drag him beyond his infancy. And then she bargained with God that if He was going to take a life, let it be hers. "I just couldn't see how I would ever take another breath if Adrian died," Mum says.

As Mum is telling me this, I realize that I can't remember a time when I did not know about Adrian, as if knowledge of him crossed the placenta and went directly into my own cells. But in every important way, I know nothing about what happened to him. When I was young, Mum would sometimes

216

spill his story, but never when she was sober and so the story grew soggy and more confused and refused to hold together. But on this late, hot morning in the Cederberg, I am forty years old and we are not drunk and Mum's narrative is relentlessly clear. Now, even as I am beginning to know the details of this story, I already know how it ends. My impulse is impossible: I want to reach back through the years and protect my young parents from what happens next.

On that hot afternoon, Dad got a message at the nickel mine from Mum. He hurried back home to find her waiting in the driveway, Vanessa in her arms. My parents drove to Bindura as fast as the Chevy would go, but Adrian was no longer at the little clinic. He had been taken by ambulance to the children's hospital in Salisbury. So now I picture my parents racing into town, Mum pale and thin at twenty-three with Vanessa on her lap, Dad helpless and unprepared at twenty-seven. They are both frantic.

Adrian was not in any of the cots in the hospital's general ward and it took some time for my parents to find him, isolated in a white cell at the end of the private wards. "He was strapped to a board, his little arms pinned down as if he were on a crucifix, with intravenous drips coming out of his head."

Mum's voice is so soft I can hardly hear her. "And he was still crying, that dry, monotonous little cry." Vanessa, aware of impending tragedy, did the only thing she could think of to make everything normal. She asked for lunch. And the nurse, matter-of-fact in the way of most Africans, told my parents not unkindly that they had a choice: they could either take Vanessa for a meal, or they could stay and watch their son die. "It was meningitis," Mum says. "And it was too late."

Now there is a long, long silence. I look out at the Cederberg Mountains, flattened gray in the noon sun. In the intensifying heat, the garden is utterly subdued. The weaver birds in the bougainvillea have given up their usual quarreling. Even the common Cape buntings have melted back into their rocky hideouts. The wind has died completely. The whole country seems crouched and serious in anticipation of the six months of dry heat to come. Somewhere in the servants' quarters a cockerel crows. Dad has his head in his hands.

Eventually Mum breaks the silence. She says, "I remember walking out of the hospital and being so shocked that the world was still there. All the jacarandas were in blossom. Salisbury looked so beautiful. The flower sellers were in Meikles Park, the aga-panthus were out, the jasmine was so sweet. And I thought, 'How can the world look normal? How are people walking around? How can everyone not understand that the world has come to an end?'"

The doctors tranquilized Mum until her grief receded to a place so deep that she was the only person who could hear it. In this way, everything about Adrian's death be-came a devastatingly slow injury, shards of hurt surfacing sometimes unexpectedly de-cades later the way pieces of shrapnel emerge from soldiers' wounds years after they have been hit. "It's the most terrible thing to go home and you walk into the nursery and all his things are there — the toys, the cot, his nappies," Mum says. "It's the most horrible thing that can happen to anyone. So I just thought, 'I've got to buck up.' And I did what I could to get on with my life."

Then Mum shakes her head. "No," she says. "No, that's not true. I didn't get on with my life. I couldn't. Vanessa kept asking, 'Where's the baby? Where's Adrian?' No one tells you how you should handle the situa-tion, and I handled it very badly. I couldn't stand it. I asked Cherry to look after Vanessa for a few days. I took more of those awful tranquilizers and I lay in a dark room with a pillow over my head. I didn't want to hear anything. I didn't want to see anything. I wanted to stop. Just stop being."

Three days after Adrian died, Dad spent half his month's wages on a two-piece suit from an Indian tailor in the second-class district. Then he drove to the children's hospital, picked up the small urn they gave him and interred Adrian's ashes at the Warren Hills Cemetery in southern Salisbury.

"All alone?" I ask.

Dad's eyes threaten to brim. "Well, it's not the sort of thing you send invitations out for."

As Adrian's ashes were closed into the wall, the season's first rain began to fall. Water pooled at my father's feet on the hard earth. It ran down his face. The suit from the second-class district shrank, the sleeves crawled up his arms, the legs receded up his calves, and blue dye ran on the red soil. Dad stood in place and memorized everything: the rangy lilac bushes, the pied crows, the cold rain on hot earth, the small and lonely grave.

A few years ago, my parents went back to look for it, the bronze marker with my brother's name on it, but along with anything else of value in that cemetery, the marker had been ripped off, melted down and sold or used for something else. I had always believed that Adrian's grave was unmarked, but it was more than that: his grave had been unmarked after the fact. In this way, Adrian is most African: a victim of circumstances, he lies anonymous in that beautiful, bloodied soil, with no date to mark either his birth or his passing. His grave as good as empty. "You can't blame desperate people for that," Dad says.

Mum looks up and her eyes are bright. "Yes, you can," she says. She is adamant. "Yes, you must."

And it seems to me that both my parents are correct. Whether out of desperation, ignorance or hostility, humans have an unerring capacity to ignore one another's sacred traditions and to defile one another's hallowed grounds: the Palawa Aborigines lost on Waternish, the Macdonalds trapped in St. Francis Cave on Eigg, the MacLeods burned in Trumpan Church, the Boers dying in British concentration camps, thousands of Kikuyu perishing during the Mau Mau, the Rucks family hacked to death in Kenya's White Highlands, Adrian's grave desecrated. Surely until all of us own and honor one another's dead, until we have admitted to our murders and forgiven one another and ourselves for what we have done, there can be no truce, no dignity and no peace.

Before the end of the next disappointing rainy season (another drought), Boofy — worn out by gin, cigarettes and disappointment — finally died of throat cancer. She left a cruelly unfinished life and — not wealth, exactly — but the impression of wealth. Wrongly assuming that my father would inherit a lawyer's bounty, Lytton-Brown settled out of court the case my parents had brought against him for his refusal to pay their bonus. My parents banked the money — there was little else to do with it; because of UDI, Rhodesian dollars could not leave the country — and a week later they crossed into Botswana via Victoria Falls and set up a tented camp on the Chobe River.

"Your mother was very brave," Dad tells me. "Your mother is a very brave lady."

So I picture them in Botswana on the banks of the Chobe: Vanessa throwing all their silver teaspoons into the river; Dad fussing with his pipe and catching fish for supper; Mum downwind of a turpentine-scented mopane campfire with tears on her cheeks. "You're all right, Tub?"

And Mum putting on a brave face. "You know how it is. Smoke gets in your eyes."

Then, singing the way she always has, out of tune but with an unerring knack of hitting the truest emotional note, "So I smile and say, when a lovely flame dies, smoke gets in your eyes. Smoke gets in your eyes."

Nicola Fuller in England

1969

Van and Bo with grandparents in Karoi. Rhodesia, circa 1973.

Mum is profoundly superstitious: she will not walk under a ladder, nor will she look at a new moon through glass. She scratches an itchy palm with wood and tosses spilled salt over her left shoulder. She won't close the windows in a thunderstorm, nor will she kill a spider. But in July 1968, for the first time in her life, she did not ritually touch the four walls of her room in Africa before embarking on the ship to England. And instead of leaving the doors open behind her, she made sure every door was firmly shut, and locked. "I didn't want to come back to Africa," she says. "Not ever."

On the ship from Africa to England she carried these things: Vanessa; the fetal me ("conceived at the Victoria Falls Casino Hotel. A bit second rate, I'm afraid"); a hangover as a result of the excellent service on the train from Salisbury to Lourenco Marques ("It was my birthday, so the Portuguese waiters brought us gallons and gallons of free wine"); a few favorite books; two hunting prints; the Wellington bronze and the Le Creuset pots.

The MS *Oranje* (later known as MS *Angelina Lauro*) was the dreariest ship Mum has ever been on. "There were a lot of Zambian miners and American missionaries on board. It was not a hilarious amount of fun." But what seems to have upset Mum even more than the dull company was that half the women on board had bought the same new dress as she had, "a shapeless thing in sludgy beige. It was all they had in Rhodesia because of sanctions — bolts and bolts of ghastly colored cotton made into one hideously unflattering pattern."

Mum sulked in her berth and wouldn't look out of her porthole. As the ship pulled out from the harbor, she turned her back on Africa and for the rest of the journey she refused to race up on deck with the other passengers whenever land was glimpsed: the faint, green blur of Kenya's coast; the hot, orange shimmer of Somalia and Sudan. And as the ship was piloted through the Suez Canal, she ate white rice and complained that the reek of the canal was giving her morning sickness. She came on deck only when England was within sight. Then she stared at the island emerging out of the thick breath of a humid summer's day, and she willed herself to feel British.

Nothing stirred.

To begin with, my parents rented a semi-detached house in Stalybridge, Cheshire, from a merchant seaman. "There was no double glazing. You could see, hear and smell everything the neighbors did." And whenever my parents tried to make the most of the long summer evenings the neighbors teased them. "There goes Gov'ment House having tea on lawn." So Mum and Dad borrowed money, bought a rundown little farm near Glossop in Derbyshire and lived in the barn. "The roof leaked, drafts blew straight through chinks in the walls, there was no electricity, no running water and no loo," Mum says. "Just a bucket in a shed out back." But the Peak District was close, "a bit of open," Mum says, and it was land beneath their feet.

Dad found what work he could in town. Mum bred rabbits, fattened chickens, fed pigs and drank a half pint of Guinness each day, paid for by the National Health. "In those days, they used to say that half a pint of Guinness a day was very good for pregnant women," Mum says.

"Are you sure?"

"Of course I'm sure. They even advertised it: 'Guinness is Good for You.'" Mum sighs. "Mind you, it didn't do much to guarantee beautiful babies. I got such a fright when they gave you to me. Black hair, yellow skin and the most impressively disagreeable expression you can possibly imagine on a brand-new baby." She narrows in on me. "Don't you sometimes feel you must have been switched at birth?"

News of my arrival reached my father very early on the morning of March 29, 1969. Dad fed the animals and dropped Vanessa off with a neighbor, whose husband, Kevin, was in the process of selling Dad a car number–plate business. The business came complete with a very hot-tempered Spanish ex-prisoner of war who both made the number plates and contributed some bona fide authority to the name, Continental Car Plates.

"Where's Kevin?" Dad asked the neighbor's wife.

"Down pub."

Dad looked at his watch. His admiration for Kevin grew exponentially. "That's very heroic of him."

Dad went down pub himself and found Kevin having a quick prebreakfast hair of the dog, but upon hearing the news that Mum had produced an offspring, Kevin slammed his pint on the bar. "Champagne!" he shouted. The workday was canceled, friends were rounded up and morning visiting hours were missed. It wasn't until two in the afternoon that Dad suddenly came to and remembered that he hadn't yet bought a present for my post-delivery Mum.

"Swift thinking," Kevin said.

So Kevin and my father had a quick one for the road and then drove around Glossop looking for a gift of some sort.

"What does Nicola go in for?" Kevin asked.

"Dogs," Dad said. "She likes dogs a lot more than she likes most people."

"So what about a puppy?"

Dad rubbed his chin. "Better not," he said. "She's likely to ignore the baby if we do that."

"Fair enough," Kevin said.

"Also culture — she's very keen on books, opera, art, that sort of thing."

Kevin looked out the window doubtfully. "Oh bollocks," he said.

Dad sank into a thoughtful reverie. "I think I'd be better able to concentrate if I had a drink in front of me," he said at last.

"Me too," Kevin said, so they swerved into the nearest pub, where they discussed further possibilities over a brandy: a horse was dismissed as too big; a China tea set was rejected as too mundane; and they both felt a night at the Proms would be expensive and noisy. "All that hollering in the Albert Hall," Kevin said. He downed his brandy and put his glass upside down on his head. Dad stared at Kevin for a moment and then he jumped to his feet. "That's it! A hat! She loves hats! How about a hat?"

"A hat?" Kevin repeated uncertainly.

"Hat and dress then," Dad said.

So the two men drove up and down the high street until they found a suitably posh women's boutique. "Top of the afternoon to you," Dad said to the woman behind the counter. "Cash customer! Do we get a discount for good behavior?"

Kevin collapsed in an armchair by the changing rooms.

"Don't worry about him," Dad told the shop assistant. "It's been a tiring day. Now what do you have in the . . ." — Dad whistled and swiveled his hips a few times — "department?"

Dad tried on several outfits, but at last the shop assistant and Kevin agreed on a short, scalloped pink mini with a matching satin pillbox hat. Then both men felt strongly that it would be a criminal waste not to give the dress a proper outing before it had to be folded up neatly in a gift box. Accordingly, they crawled around a few more pubs, picking up champagne, flowers and cigars along the way, until at last they calculated it must be getting close to afternoon visiting hours. "And don't spare the horses," Dad said. "We don't want to be late."

There was a confused moment in the car park of the nursing home while Kevin and Dad debated the merits of my father's showing up in the maternity ward in the dress. "It's a bit worse for the wear. Perhaps you'd better get back into your suit," Kevin suggested. But the dress's buttons and zips defeated both men, and in the end, it was decided to leave well enough alone.

Mum shakes her head. "You can just imagine," she says. "Your dad comes bursting into the ward in a pink minidress, arms full of flowers and champagne, puffing away on a cigar with a very drunk Kevin weaving behind him."

"Let's have a party!" Dad shouted.

"For heaven's sake, this is a nursing home," Mum hissed. "Keep it down."

"Sorry," Dad said, momentarily chastened. And then sotto voce, "Hallelujah! Hallelujah! Hallelujah! Hallelujah! Hallelujah! For the Lord God Omnipotent reigneth! Hallelujah!"

Mum held her hands to her ears. "No, Tim, no. No singing. And for God's sake, *not* 'The Hallelujah Chorus.'"

The door slapped open and the matron stormed in to see what all the fuss was about. "How do you do?" Dad said, bowing. The matron froze in her tracks. Dad put a rose behind his ear and began to do the samba. "Work all night on a drink of rum," he sang, waving a cigar in the air. "Daylight come and me wan' go home."

"I thought I was going to get hell," Mum says. "But Matron got one whiff of Dad's cigar and she cried, 'Oh, that's so romantic, just like Barbara Cartland.'" Then the woman in the bed next to Mum's burst into tears because her husband wasn't romantic. "He was a cotton-mill worker and he had piles," Mum says. "When he came to visit, he had to sit on one of those special cushions with a hole in the middle of it." Dad poured champagne for everyone.

"No one thought to fetch me from the nursery?" I ask.

"Oh no," Mum says. "No, no, no, you'd been safely bundled off by then."

For two more winters, Mum and Dad stuck it out in Derbyshire. Mum's rabbits got out of their cages and bred as rabbits will. So Dad told a nearby farmer that he could have the farms' rabbit-shooting privileges in exchange for a springer spaniel puppy, Che. ("Shoot as *many* as you can," Dad begged.) Then a fox terrier showed up on the doorstep, shivering and emaciated, so that was Jacko. And finally, Mum was given a goat whose owner had multiple sclerosis. "So how could I say no? Anyway, the bloody thing was supposed to be housebroken and tame. He was nothing of the sort. He ran all over the house spraying pellets everywhere. He ate whatever he could get his teeth into. We tried giving him a basket to sleep in, but he was used to beds. And he howled if you left him outside."

But however much my parents tried to ensure a colorfully chaotic life for themselves, there was an underlying sense that as long as they stayed in England, they would always have to be the source of their own drama. Moreover, beyond a weekly session at the local pub with Kevin and a few other friends, there was no one with whom to do anything. "Margot Fonteyn came to Manchester," Mum says, "and I had to go to the ballet with the milkman's wife. It was very kind of her to come along, but I don't think she ever recovered from the shock of seeing Rudolph Nureyev in tights." Mum blinks at me rapidly. "Well, it was a little eye-popping."

It rained all spring. Then the summer was dreary too. Gradually, the droughty desperation of Rhodesia receded in my parents' minds. Instead of the snakes at Berry's Post, they now remembered Tabatha chasing Vanessa around a wide lawn; instead of waiting a whole season for rain that never came, they now remembered the hot plash of the Rhodesian sun against their skin; instead of the isolation precipitated by Ian Smith's Unilateral Declaration of Independence (the international sanctions, the rationed petrol, the bolts of sludgy cotton made into identical shapeless dresses, the state censorship), they now remembered the self-reliant camaraderie of Rhodesians and the astonishing kindness of strangers.

So before another winter could trap them in a frigid grip of chores and gloom, they culled the chickens, butchered the pigs, sent the goat to the knacker's yard, rented out the barn (recently equipped with flush loos, electricity, less-leaky walls), sold the number-plate business (complete with hot-tempered Spaniard), and rolled up the farm's turf to sell as lawn. Then they went down pub one last time and announced that they were moving south. "We didn't say how far south," Mum admits. "We didn't dare. Rhodesia was a completely illegal, ostracized country. Very, very frowned upon."

"Then why did you go back?" I ask.

"Well," Mum says, "we still had those Rhodesian dollars in the bank from the Lytton-Brown settlement — a few thousand or whatever it was. That was one thing. And it was Africa, that was the main thing — we wanted to go back to Africa. We longed for the warmth and freedom, the real open spaces, the wild animals, the sky at night."

For their journey my parents packed up the two dogs, Mum's collection of books, the two hunting prints, linens, towels, the bronze cast of Wellington (now missing its stirrup leathers) and the Le Creuset pots. Because of international sanctions against the country, Rhodesia had to be reached circuitously. Dad flew ahead via Malawi to find a job and somewhere to live. Mum followed on the SS *Uganda* from Southampton to Cape Town. "Oh, it was a wonderful little ship," Mum says. "There were blue leather chairs in the wood-paneled smoking room and deliciously evocative oil paintings on the walls. And on either side of the chimneypiece, there was a set of enormous elephant tusks, a gift from the king of the Baganda to his country's namesake ship. It was very romantic."

And if that was not enough, Mum befriended the most glamorous passenger on board. "Paddy Latimer was en route to join her husband, who had a farm in South Africa. She had three little girls, one little boy, she was pregnant and she still looked simply gorgeous." As the two women waved good-bye to England at Southampton, they realized they both had dogs. "Which was a tremendous bond, of course, so that was it," Mum says. "We did everything together after that. Well, almost everything." Paddy was the daughter of a ship-building family, "so she would swan up to eat at the top table with the captain and I'd be stuck with the rest of the povo." But for breakfast and lunch and for the rest of the day, Paddy joined Mum.

In the mornings, the two women walked their dogs on the deck. They read, they wrote letters, they sunbathed. After lunch, they took languid siestas beneath the shade of days-old newspapers. Then in the afternoons they lazily plotted the world's easiest costumes for the inevitable, dreaded Fancy Dress Party into which they reckoned they had to enter at least one child each. "Fig leaves," Mum says. "What could be easier? So her little James went as Adam and you went as Eve, and you were terribly sweet, toddling hand in hand, fig leaves over your bits and pieces. I think the judges were quite impressed until James swiveled his leaves around — one on each hip — and started to engage in seriously unBiblical behavior with whatever was left hanging out."

The farther south the ship sailed, the more Mum rejoiced. As Africa swelled into view, she pinned herself to the railings of the deck and felt the dampness of the last three years lift from her shoulders. When a hint of shimmering purple ribbon on the horizon bespoke Kenya, she held her face to the west and tried to inhale the perfect equatorial light. And as the ship veered around the tip of Africa, Mum held me up to the earthy, wood-fire-spiced air. A hot African wind blew my black bowl cut into a halo. "Smell that," Mum whispered in my ear. "That's home."

NICOLA FULLER IN RHODESIA: ROUND TWO

Bo's children on a visit back to southern Africa. Great Zimbabwe, Zimbabwe, 2001.

To begin with, there are these scattered and unattached recollections: a snake in the honeysuckle creeper behind our house; Vanessa perspiring in her school uniform, valiantly persisting in her refusal to read; a rustling carpet of dead insects being swept off the veranda each morning; a lamb being slaughtered in a kraal under some eucalyptus trees where I hear, for the first time, Afrikaans being spoken; the taste of roasted maize in the compound where the language is Shona. (And words from both Shona and Afrikaans breaking into my everyday English: nyoka, lekker, maiwe! voetsek, huku.)

But my first consistent memory is of a farmhouse outside the small town of Karoi. "A lot of rooms strung together under a hot tin roof," I say. "And wasn't it flat and very dry, and the lawn was full of paper thorns?"

Mum puts down her teacup. "Well, yes. It wasn't much of a house, but the farmer who owned the place was very kind and generous and he let us stay there rent free." Mum gives me a look. "*And* he used to have terribly wild parties, something to do with blowing a feather across a sheet until all your clothes were off. We never understood it because we were very innocent, weren't we Tim?"

"What's that?" Dad says.

"INNOCENT," Mum shouts, "WE WERE VERY INNOCENT."

Dad lights his pipe. "Oh yes," he says. "That's right." A cloud of smoke wraps around his head. "Absolutely."

The three of us are sitting under the Tree of Forgetfulness on a Sunday afternoon one recent May, in what passes for autumn in the Zambezi Valley. I've chosen this time of year to travel from Wyoming to visit my parents because although it's still hot, it's not unbearably so. Between the extremes of the seasons (the earth neither flooded nor parched), their farm has taken on a genuinely bucolic air: geese and sheep cropping rhythmically around the fish ponds; an occasional cockerel from the nearby village hollering to his hens (the sound reminds me of childhood afternoons, waking up after a heat-drugged siesta); birds squabbling at the fruit feeder in Mum's garden. "Look at that," she says, "a black-collared barbet." She cocks her head and talks to him, "Too-puddley, too-puddley, too-puddley, too-puddley. . . ."

And then, as if still addressing the bird, Mum returns to her memories, "Well, we never planned to stay in Karoi anyway. It was already too taken, too settled for us, wasn't it, Tim? We wanted land that came with a swath of wilderness, somewhere a bit more out of the ordinary." So on Sundays Dad brought the weekly newspaper home and my parents laid the classifieds out on the dining room table next to a map of Rhodesia and they searched for a farm the size and shape of the dream they had in their heads.

By 1930, all Rhodesia's land had been officially apportioned by the colonial government. Unsurprisingly, designated European areas coincided roughly with the high-rainfall, fertile areas; Tribal Trust Lands lay more or less in the dry periphery; and the tiny allotment of Native Purchase Areas were farther away in the oppressively hot, tsetse-fly–prone zones. European settlers gave no sign that they considered their allotment as either immoral or dangerously unsustainable. For one thing, there was a very strong sense that God had given the settlers two holy thumbs-up ("Onward Christian Soldiers" was a popular enough hymn to wear out the relevant keys on Protestant church organs across the country). For another thing, many whites considered blacks so childishly inferior that taking their land was considered a justified occupation of virgin soil. "I don't wish to be unkind," Rhodesian prime minister Ian Smith said in 1970, "but sixty years ago Africans were uncivilized savages, walking around in their skins."

Smith and his followers seemed determined to deny the country an African history prior to the arrival of Europeans. They rejected, for example, the evidence of what the Rhodesians called Zimbabwe Ruins, a complex of conical towers and massive stone walls in the southeastern part of the country concluded to be the royal enclosure of a medieval Shona empire. Undulating over eighteen hundred acres, it is the largest ancient structure south of the Sahara. Archaeological excavations uncovered shards of pottery from China, and Arabian beads pointing to an undeniable level of civilization. To get around this awkward fact, Smith's government put enormous pressure on archaeologists to deny that the structures could ever have been constructed by black Africans. At least one prominent archaeologist, Peter Garlake, was forced to leave the country when he refused to do so.

Nor did the Rhodesian government appear to register the irony that, for such avowed anti-Communists — "The war against Communism is ultimately a religious war in which the very thing that makes life worth living is at stake"* — their policy of land allocation put much of the country, namely, the Tribal Trust Lands, into communal ownership. By default, this forced millions of black Rhodesians into massive collectives

*Ivor Benson, Ian Smith's official propagandist.

where their every move could be monitored and controlled by an increasingly militaristic and paranoid government. Still, most of the two hundred fifty thousand or so white Rhodesians were unwilling or disinclined to question an official government policy that gave them preferential treatment over six million blacks, instead preferring to believe that theirs was a just and justifiable life of privilege. Critics accused these whites of belonging to the Mushroom Club: "Kept in the dark and fed horseshit."

So, "Shangri-la!" Mum announced triumphantly one Sunday, stopping her finger on its way down the real estate page. She read aloud, "Robandi Farm; seven hundred acres for sale in the Burma Valley." She named the price — reasonable enough — so together my parents looked at the map. From what they could tell, Robandi was a handful of miles (as the bird flies) from Umtali, a small city on Rhodesia's eastern border with Portuguese-controlled Mozambique. "Oh!" Mum cried. "Portuguese wine, stinky cheese, piri piri prawns! We must have this farm."

Phone calls were patched through various telephone exchanges until at last the line crackled with the voice of an estate agent in Umtali. He told my parents that the farm's executor was an Italian farmer by the name of John Parodi — he lived in the Burma Valley and he could give my parents a tour of the place if they were interested. "Interested?!" Mum cried. "Of course we're interested." She hung up the phone and turned to Dad, her eyes shining. "Italian!" she cried. "I do think that shows the proper romantic spirit, don't you?"

A day or two later, my parents left Karoi before dawn and drove across the country. Along the way, in preparation for meeting the farm's executor, Mum dusted off the handful of Italian phrases she had picked up over the years. "Ciao, come stai?" she attempted as my parents drove across the Angwa River. "Il mio nome è Nicola," she practiced as they skirted the Inyanga Highlands. "Arrivederci!" she cried as Christmas Pass faded into the rearview mirror and the car dipped into the jacaranda-lined main street of Umtali.

"For heaven's sake, Tub, are we going to buy a farm, or are you planning to run away with this chap?" Dad asked.

Mum shot Dad one of her ravishing smiles. "We shall see what we shall see," she said.

At the southern end of Umtali, Mum and Dad stopped for a cold beer and a plate of eggs and bacon at Brown's Hotel. As they were leaving, they asked directions to the Burma Valley from the handful of diehards at the bar. "Oh no! No, no, no, you don't want to go down there," a man said. "They're all wife swappers, drunks and madmen."

Dad raised a hand. "Two for the road then, please, barman," he said.

My parents drove out of town through the second-class district, where the Indians had their warehouses, tailor shops and stores; under the railway bridge; past the paper mill, pungent with the scent of freshly peeled pine; and around the knot of hills surrounding Umtali (Kumakomoyo, the local Manyika called it, "the place of many mountains"). The tarmac ended and my parents bumped onto a dirt road in the Zamunya Tribal Trust Land, with its bony cattle, its ribby red earth and its goat-shredded trees. Then they crossed an enormous cattle grid and suddenly the barren world of Zimunya lifted away. What took its place were a rich, humid bowl of jungle and a wide basin of deeply fertile farmland.

"We loved the valley instantly," Mum says. "That jungle as you dropped down into it, those huge trees with wonderful birds clattering away in the canopy." My parents stopped the car at the bottom of the escarpment to let the brakes cool. To the north lay the mist-shouldered Vumba Mountains. To the south ran the distant Chimanimani range. And opposite them were the hot, buffalo-bean covered Himalaya Hills (the actual Himalayas having been seen by the first white settler of Burma Valley, a *pukka*-pukka sahib from India). "It was all so lush, so picturesque, so life affirming," Mum says. She threw her hands above her head and spun around and around to the chorus of tree frogs and the shrilling of insects. "It's perfect!" she cried. "Yippee! Hurrah!"

It was almost noon by the time they found John Parodi's farm. "A little piece of Italy in all its details," Mum says. An avenue of Mediterranean cypresses led up from the tobacco barns; dairy cattle grazed in knee-deep pastures on either side of the road; a bright bay horse was attended by white egrets; the whitewashed farmhouse was topped with a red tile roof; Ionic columns held up the veranda.

My parents were greeted in the brick-paved courtyard by a maid and shown into a large sitting room, at the center of which was a gurgling fountain. Ferns spilled off the bookshelves and pressed against the windows, creating filtered green light. The whole house was redolent with olive oil and freshly baked bread. "Che bello!" Mum cried, and at that moment John Parodi strode into the room. "Oh, you know what he was like," Mum says. "Those shoulders! That passion!"

So I picture John on that steaming October morning, oxlike in his khaki bush jacket with his salted black hair combed back to expose a sun-burnished forehead and formidable winged eyebrows. He embraced my parents, kissing Mum on both cheeks, pounding Dad between the shoulder blades, shouting English with a thick Italian accent. "You must sit! Sit!"

My parents sat.

John poured glasses of liqueur — "all different colors, like liquid jewels," Mum says — and they drank to one another's health.

"Cent'anni!"

"Mud in your eye!"

Then my parents were led from the seemingly subterranean sitting room to an airy, high-ceilinged dining room, from which French doors opened onto the veranda, where dogs lay curled in the shade and cats cleaned themselves under potted orange trees. "Just like in Roma," Mum observed happily. Lunch was served, Portuguese wine flowed out of basket-covered bottles and more liqueurs arrived. John raised his glass and roared that the world was both beautiful and heartbreaking. My mother bawled back her hearty agreement. They became drunker, they yelled louder and Mum acquired an intensely strong Italian accent of her own.

"He told us over lunch the many tragedies of his love life — two or three at least. Things are a little vague, I'm afraid — those liqueurs were *very* alcoholic — but I think his first wife might have died. Or maybe she ran away — something like that." So John apparently sent to Italy for Elsa, the striking and spirited daughter of his unrequited first love. "I'm not sure but I suppose Elsa and John must have fallen in love and maybe Italy after the war was dreary. I really don't know." In any case, Elsa came out to Africa, and shortly afterward, she and John must have been married. In due course they had two children: a daughter, Madeline (a couple of years older than Vanessa), and a son, Giovanni (my age). "And it should have been happily ever after except then Elsa fell for the handsome, charming tobacco farmer next door." What my mother doesn't say, but we all know, is that Elsa and the handsome tobacco farmer were caught in the tobacco barns one evening, in flagrante dilecto. "Can you imagine?"

"The bloody bitch and the bloody bastard!" John bellowed, waving his fist in the direction of the offending neighbor, the straying wife. "I shoot them!"

A clap of thunder broke above the house, and an afternoon storm rolled across the valley. "Amore!" Mum shouted, raising her glass to the sky.

"Amore!" John replied.

It need hardly be said that by the time my parents finally climbed into John's pickup and bumped across the valley to be shown Robandi Farm they had begun to see the world in distinctly rainbow shades. "The whole place was freshly washed in rain. The flamboyant trees on the driveway were in bloom," Mum says. "The Persian lilacs were dripping nectar." And the garden, lightly soaked, gave off the scents of frangipani and red earth. "We told John we must have the farm," Mum says. "He agreed that it should be ours. That was it. I think we signed some sort of agreement on the spot."

"Wait," I say. "You didn't walk around the fields first? You didn't feel the soil? You didn't inspect the barns or check the water supply?"

Mum gives me a look, as if I am the murderer of fairy stories. "We didn't feel it was

249

necessary. There was such a pretty view across the valley to John Parodi's farm and beyond that to Mozambique, wasn't there, Tim?"

"What's that?" Dad says.

"A TERRIFIC VIEW OF MOZAM-BIQUE," Mum shouts. "FROM THE HOUSE!"

So my parents borrowed money to buy the farm, and we moved from Karoi to the Burma Valley (two children, three dogs, two cats, one horse, some china, the linen, Wellington, the two hunting prints, a second-hand treadle sewing machine and the Le Creuset pots). Seen without the beneficial filter of every different color liqueur in John Parodi's liquor cabinet, Robandi was rockier than would have been ideal and it was in a rain shadow. The flamboyant trees seethed with termite nests and nothing would grow under them. The house, which had looked mysterious beneath a canopy of fiery red blooms, was, on closer inspection, a dreary bunker. "But it was our own farm in Africa." Mum sighs. "And we were so happy, so proud, so sure this was where we would spend the rest of our lives."

Mum painted the outside of the house an apricot-peachy color. She brought out the treadle sewing machine and made curtains out of mattress ticking. She hung Irish linen tea cloths and china plates on the walls to augment the hunting prints, and she planted the garden with vegetation guaranteed to thrive on the maximum amount of neglect. Finally, she filled up the swimming pool, but without an electric pump and expensive chemicals, it quickly turned green and in a short while, played host to scores of frogs, a family of ducks, some geese and the occasional Nile monitor. "Well, there you go," Mum said, squinting at the overall effect of the garden, the pink house, the verdant swimming pool. "Very soothing and picturesque, no?"

At night we ate Mum's colorful vegetables fresh from the garden and her tough home-raised chickens tenderized into fragrant curries in the Le Creuset pots. "Ah, fantastico!" Mum took a sip of the cheapest possible Portuguese wine, and she clinked her glass against Dad's, "Here's to us," she said, "there're none like us. And if there were, they're all dead." And for a moment in that spluttering candlelight, with their two growing daughters, their pack of dogs, their one difficult horse, their wild swimming pool, it looked as if Mum and Dad might be happy here forever: Dad with his farm to shape into

a southern African version of Douthwaite;
Mum with her life to shape into something
biography worthy.

And then, just a few months after we
moved to Robandi, something happened
halfway around the world that changed
everything. In April 1974, revolutionaries
marched through the streets of Lisbon holding red carnations to symbolize their socialist ideology. In the aftermath of the coup,
Portuguese colonies in sub-Saharan Africa
were immediately granted their independence and a million Portuguese citizens fled
from those territories. Mozambique's new
Marxist-Leninist FRELIMO government
announced it was supporting the ZANLA
guerilla soldiers who were fighting majority
rule in Rhodesia. In retaliation, the Rhodesian government funded RENAMO, an
anti-Communist rebel army in central Mozambique. The border between Rhodesia
and Mozambique was closed, and between
the two countries, a cordon sanitaire (literally "quarantine corridor" but actually a
minefield) was built a few miles above our
farm.

Dad was conscripted into the Rhodesian Army Reserves and Mum voluntarily
joined the Police Reservists. She became a
Red Cross emergency responder. Every few

weeks, Dad put on his camouflage uniform and disappeared with six other Burma Valley farmers to fight in the Himalayas. Mum learned to run the farm in his absence. They slept with an Uzi and an FN rifle next to the bed, they ate with Browning Hi-Power pistols on their side plates and they taught Vanessa and me how to shoot to kill. They put sandbags in front of the windows and surrounded the farmhouse with security fencing. We bought an old Land Rover, mine-proofed it and named it Lucy. And Mum came up with her Olé! war cry, which we sang on Wednesday and Saturday evenings on our way to the Burma Valley Club, where Mum danced on the bar (gorgeous with her long auburn hair, her pale green eyes).

But in those early days, the war was more like the unwelcome threat of bad weather than something perpetually violent. "The big thing was to pull up your socks and carry on as effortlessly as possible," Mum says. She was scornful of the ten thousand whites who left the country: "The chicken run," we called it. And she had no tolerance for those who said black rule was inevitable. "Over my dead body," she said. "Life must go on."

So she taught Vanessa and me proper elocution for hours and hours. "There," we said, trying not to flatten the end of the word. "Women," we said, as if the word had only *i*'s and two *m*'s. "Nice," we said, smiling over the *i* instead of rhyming it with "farce." We rescued several dogs. We were given another horse. Vanessa was packed off to boarding school in Umtali. ("She pretends not to be able to read," Mum told her teacher, "but she really knows quite a lot of Shakespeare.")

I was given correspondence school lessons at home with an emphasis on what my mother considered the sacred arts of storytelling, and after lunch, before we both fell asleep in the limb-deadening afternoon heat, Mum read to me: *The Jungle Book, Winnie-the-Pooh, The Wind in the Willows.* In the cool evenings, Mum sat with tea on her lap, eyes half closed. "Story of the Week," she would demand. And I would tell her, "This week I rode through the river on my horse with one eye."

"Hm." Mum would smile. "*Splashed* is better than *rode,* don't you think? *I splashed through the river on my one-eyed horse, the dogs paddling next to me. . . .* How about something like that?"

Then in the humid November of 1975, Mum felt suddenly overwhelmed by a familiar nausea. By early August of the following year, she was heavily pregnant. "A week or two left I would have said," Doctor Mitchell told her, frowning. "And in this condition, must you be all the way out there on that farm? It's not safe." Almost on cue, the war suddenly escalated. On the night of August 11, 1976, the Mozambican army launched a mortar attack into the southern suburbs of Umtali. Vanessa — at boarding school — was herded with the other girls downstairs, where they were pushed onto the concrete floor and had mattresses thrown on them with such hurried force that some of them ended up with contusions. When she came home for the weekend, I admired her bruised knees, the egg on her forehead, and bombarded her with questions. Was she frightened? Did she see any dead bodies? Did she see a terrorist? But Vanessa only looked self-protectively bored, and Mum said, "Don't go on and on and on about it, Bobo. It's over now, isn't it?"

The Rhodesian government issued thousands of prewritten air letters for white families to send to friends and relatives overseas with institutionally authoritative language that nonetheless accurately mirrored our internal denial: "No doubt you are worried about the situation in Rhodesia, particularly in view of all the sensational headlines and horrific articles which appear in the press," the letter began. "What much of the world press does not wish to print are the true facts about Rhodesia. That she has weathered the last ten years so well, in terms of internal peace, productivity, growth and racial harmony, despite the effects of boycotts and sanctions."

In the days following the reported mailing of more than fifteen thousand of these letters, ambushes on white Rhodesian farmers and government forces became more common and the artillery even more deadly, and whatever else this was, it wasn't a scrappy little bush war anymore. Doctor Mitchell was adamant, "Get into town, for God's sake, Nicola," he told Mum. "And stay in town until that child is born."

"But you have mortars there too," Mum objected.

"Yes, but at least we also have a hospital."

So with Dad off fighting in the Himalayas, Mum and I moved into town and stayed with friends and waited and waited for the baby to arrive. "I would have been bored half to death," Mum says. "But luckily *The Rocky Horror Picture Show* had finally found its way to the Rainbow Theatre, so I watched that at least three times." And on August 28, Olivia Jane Fuller was born in the Umtali General Hospital — dark curls, full Garrard lips and the most extraordinary violet-blue eyes anyone had ever seen. The nurses called one another from different stations to show off Olivia's eyes and they took her to visit the wounded convalescents in other wards. In this suddenly very bloody war, Olivia seemed an unlikely and almost redemptive thing of beauty.

From her window in the maternity ward, Mum could see the casualties arriving from the front lines in red dust–covered army trucks and Land Rovers and ambulances (all the incoming soldiers to this particular hospital were white; black soldiers fighting for Rhodesia were sent to the hospital for black people, proving that you can die for a cause for which you won't necessarily be saved). "I do remember those wounded troops. They were so young, some of them, they looked like schoolboys," Mum says. "Their razor haircuts fresh enough that the sunburn hadn't yet had time to scorch the white off their necks." Mum heard the boys calling for their mothers and she cradled Olivia on her shoulder. "It's all right, little girl," she told the baby. "It's all right."

When Olivia was a week old, we brought her home through Zamunya Tribal Trust Land and into the valley, escorted by a convoy of soldiers and minesweepers. Seeing the new baby, the soldiers were especially assiduous in their work that day. "Her eardrums won't take it if there's an incident hey," the convoy leader told Mum. He cradled Olivia's downy head in his gun-oily hand, incongruously tender in his camouflage, his belts of ammunition, his war-weary boots. "Agh shame," he said awkwardly, as if gentleness was something nearly forgotten on his tongue. "She's so sweet — look at those eyes."

And this nearly forgotten gentleness enveloped Robandi too. There were still the stripped guns on newspaper in the sitting room, the antigrenade defenses outside the windows, the Agric Alert radio crackling security updates morning and evening: "Oscar Papa two-eight, Oscar Papa two-eight, this is HQ. How do you read? Over." But there was also the routine comfort of boiled bottles in the kitchen; a curtain of white nappies on the washing line behind the house; Mum reading in bed late into the morning with the baby asleep against her neck. And in the evenings, instead of the dread news with reports of casualties and attacks and counterattacks, Mum took the wireless out onto the veranda, tuned it to the classical-and-oldies station and slow-waltzed Olivia into the garden, around the frangipani tree. "Everybody loves my baby," she sang. "But my baby don't love nobody but me."

In January 1977, I joined Vanessa at boarding school in Umtali. "Good luck, Bobo," Mum told me. "Be good for your teachers, listen to your matrons and try not to be homesick." She picked up my dachshund. "I'm sure Jason will miss you terribly." She waggled Jason's paw in my direction. "Won't you, Jason King?" Olivia stayed home with Mum and with Violet, the nanny. Once a month, Mum and Dad came to fetch us for the weekend and we were escorted back to the valley by a convoy of security vehicles and minesweepers. All the way home Vanessa and I fought over who would have Olivia on her lap.

"I'm eldest."

"Ja, but she likes me better."

"No, she doesn't."

"Look, I can make her laugh."

"Don't tickle her, she doesn't like it."

"Ja, she does."

"Doesn't."

Until Mum (sitting in the front with her Uzi pointed out the window) swiveled around and threatened to swat both of us unless we settled down, shut up and looked after the baby. "Are you paying attention?" she asked, and we both knew what that meant. After that we got serious and put Olivia on the seat between us, below the level of a window so that if we were ambushed, a bullet would have to go through the Land Rover door *and* one of us before it could ever reach our baby. There was an unspoken rule. If we were all going to die, it would be in this order: Dad, Mum, Vanessa, me and then unthinkably last but only over all of our dead bodies, Olivia.

OLIVIA

After the drought-breaking storms of October, November usually brings steady afternoon showers, and with that predictable rain there is the returning hope that this year will be better. Mbudzi, the Shona call it, "month of goat fertility." The veldt lights up with a simmer of fresh growth, like pale green flames; wood smoke and dust are washed from the sky; white storks and black Abdim's storks return from their European holidays. So when Mum says, "It must have been November on Robandi," I imagine all of these hopeful things, but I also think of the perennial hopelessness of that farm, the way we always seemed to be at least one rainy season behind making a profit.

"Yes, it must have been November," Mum says. "And it was very hot, very humid, so I decided to leave Olivia with Violet at the house, just for an hour or so. Dad wanted to show me something at the seedbeds."

Mum looks at her work-worn hands. "I was very involved with the farm, you see." And I envision Mum as she was then, with her hair tucked behind her ears in the tobacco fields; or sweating on the receiving end of a calving cow; or riding her horse across the star grass, her Uzi seven pounds and seven ounces across her belly, pocking marks into the saddle's pommel with its stubby barrel. "I had to run the whole place single-handed when Dad was off fighting," she says.

By November 1977, Dad was thirty-seven, but war costs men and it costs money, so every year the Rhodesian government raised our taxes and they upped the age of conscription — all white males under the age of sixty were subject to call-up; younger white men spent twenty-five or thirty weeks a year in the army in six-week increments. Mum paddles the fingers on both hands and counts them off, her lips moving. "I think Dad was forty by the time the war ended. Forty but very fit, weren't you, Tim?"

"Sick of it," Dad says.

"Yes, but in *marvelous* shape," Mum says.

The tobacco seedbeds were on the far end of the farm, four or five miles from the house. I picture them now, rows of black plastic–covered beds on the edge of the field above the gully that sliced the farm in two. The soil here was pale and a little sandy. Baboons used to live in the msasa forest around this field, foraying into the open in the evenings. The odd duiker or bushbuck still came through from the Himalayas, and once or twice a leopard. So when Mum caught movement in the trees out of the corner of her eye, her initial reaction was not one of alarm. "I thought maybe an animal," she says.

But then the movement stepped out of the shadows into the bright sun and resolved into two men, dressed in the uniform worn by FRELIMO. "Two terrorists," my mother says, "very scruffy and desperate looking. They were each shouldering an AK47 and their shirts were dripping with grenades. One was limping badly." Mum shakes her head. "My mind went wild. I thought, 'My God, they're going to kill us in broad daylight. And then they'll go to the house and kill the baby.' We'd all seen the pictures of what the terrs had done — maimed and murdered children. God, my skin went absolutely marble cold. It was terrifying, wasn't it, Tim."

"Pretty horrible," Dad agrees.

Mum makes a fist. "But I'll tell you what — your father was so cool. He didn't panic at all." Her eyes are shining. "They say you can take the measure of a man by how he behaves at gunpoint, and I think there's a lot of truth to that."

My father watched the two men walk toward the Land Rover, the one barely able to bear weight on his leg. Dad took his revolver off his belt and put it on my mother's knee. "Get into the driver's seat," he told her. He lit a cigarette, slowly opened the Land Rover door and got out. The two terrorists kept coming toward my father, their hands lifted slightly away from their sides. Dad never took his eyes off them, but he continued to speak quietly to my mother. "Nothing's going to happen," he told her. "But if it does, fetch Olivia and get the hell off the farm. Don't look back." Then he began to walk toward the terrorists, openly unarmed.

My mother slid over from the passenger's side into the driver's seat and held the gun. She prayed silently, "Please God, not Tim. Not Tim." And then, "Please God, not the baby. Not the baby. Not the baby." She watched Dad's back, a dark stain of sweat growing between his shoulder blades. He threw his cigarette onto the ground, and squashed it dead with the toe of his velts-koen. Then he looked up, as if only just noticing the two men. "Yes, boys," he said. "Anything I can do for you?"

For a moment nothing happened. And then the limping man sank to his knees. "Baas, we're pseudo ops."

My father glanced over his shoulder at my mother. "It's okay, Tub," he said. "They're on our side."

"We need water, we need food," the limping man said. He lifted his trouser leg to reveal a gunshot in his ankle, badly infected and smelling of gangrene in that damp heat. "Please, baas, I need assistance."

My father looked at the men for a moment. "You bastards had better be who you say you are," he said quietly. He lit three cigarettes at once, handed one to each of the men and kept one for himself. Then he turned back to my mother and in a loud, reassuringly normal voice told her, "Bring the first aid kit, Tub. We've got a bit of a situation here."

Mum got out of the Land Rover, shaking with spent adrenaline. She went around to the far side of the vehicle where she could not be seen and sank onto her heels. Then she took a deep breath, got her first aid kit, walked into the bright rain-clean sunlight and did what she could for the man's ankle; swabbed it with iodine, retrieved what grit and bone fragments she could and wrapped it with a supporting bandage. "We sent them on their way after an hour or so," Dad says. "And afterward, when we phoned the police to report the incident, they told us RENAMO operatives were using our farm as a stopover on their way in and out of Mozambique. So then we knew. Mostly they came after dark; they slept in the barns and they were gone before dawn. They were self-sufficient — on the whole didn't ask for food or water. We didn't often see them unless, like that time, they were wounded and needed help, and then we'd hear them in the shateen — 'Maiwe! Maiwe!' — and you'd know some poor bastard had been hit and that he'd dragged himself back over the minefield, and we were their first chance of help." Dad shakes his head as if trying to dislodge the sound of that cry, "Maiwe! Maiwe!"

For a long time it's very quiet under the Tree of Forgetfulness. Then one of the dogs at Mr. Zalu's house begins to bark and my parents' dogs spill out into the darkness in answer, hackles stiff with suspicion. Mum's geese honk. Rose beetles crack against the lightbulbs above our heads and spin on their backs at our feet. Dad relights his pipe and puffs on it for a moment. "Well," he says at last, "the only people who think war is a glorious game are the bloody fools who've never had to be on the pointy end of it."

A month later, a bus detonated a land mine on its way through the Burma Valley. Then, just before Christmas, up in the Himalayas, Dad and the rest of his patrol were dropped off by helicopter to find a group of terrorists suspected of attempting an attack on the Leopard Rock Hotel the night before. "It wasn't much fun," Dad says, "like looking for a bloody wounded buffalo in jesse bush." In the Tribal Trust Lands there were daily reports of guerillas in the taverns and kraals waiting to ambush farmers on their way into town. Near the Davises' house there was a contact between guerillas and security forces and the sound of gunfire echoed across the valley so that it was hard to distinguish where the fighting was.

So on the morning of January 9, 1978, Mum and Dad weighed their options. Our school fees were due, which meant Mum and Dad needed to take a slaughtered steer into the township on the edge of Umtali and scrape together enough money from the sale of meat to pay the bursar. On top of that, Vanessa had undergone a sudden growth spurt, and she needed a new pair of school shoes.

Mum bit the inside of her lip. "Safest and best," she said, "to leave Bobo and Olivia at Mazonwe with Rena, don't you think?" She looked at the steer, fly-attracting and taking up more than all the room in the back of the Land Rover. "Nicer for the little ones, yes?" Mum strapped the Uzi across her chest, Dad shouldered his FN rifle and we all climbed into the Land Rover, hot and coppery with the smell of the steer's blood.

"I'm going to get shoes and you're not," Vanessa said to me.

"Don't tease Bobo," Mum said.

Vanessa pulled a face at me and mouthed, "I'm going to town. I'm going to town. I'm going to town!"

I pulled a face at Vanessa and mouthed, "I'll see Aunty Rena. I'll see Aunty Rena. I'll see Aunty Rena!"

Rena Viljeon, our favorite neighbor, was a kind and practical Scottish nurse married to an Afrikaner farmer. They had four children (also favorites), all older than Vanessa and me (their eldest son was eighteen and in the Rhodesian Special Forces), and they owned the local grocery store a couple of farms west of Robandi. The store was a child's dream: salty with dried fish and bright with sweets, soap and beads. On the veranda of the store, there was always a tailor, strips of cloth whipping through his fingers as his feet treadled: "Ka-thunka, ka-thunka, ka-thunka."

On that rainy-season morning, the sun fresh and bright through the washed sky, Olivia and I were dropped off with Aunty Rena. We stood at the security fence and waved at the Land Rover carrying Vanessa, Mum, Dad and the chopped-up steer into Umtali. Mum leaned out the window, the wind whipping her auburn hair into her mouth. "Be good and help Aunty Rena look after Olivia!" she shouted. We watched the Land Rover turn right at the end of the road, Mum's Uzi and Dad's FN rifle poking out of the window against the worst that the war could throw at them, and then we turned back to the store.

In those days, it took more than an hour to get into town — the convoys were slow, following the minesweepers. Dad dropped Vanessa and Mum at the OK Bazaar and went into the markets in the African part of town. Mum and Vanessa each had a sausage roll and a Coke at Mitchell the Baker (brother of Mitchell the doctor) and then went shopping for school shoes at the Bata on Main Street. It was here, in the early afternoon, that the local member in charge of the Umtali Police found them, Mum bent over Vanessa's stocking-clad foot, a brown lace-up in her hand. "Nicola?" he said.

Mum looked up, a half smile on her lips. "What are you doing here, Malcolm?" But seeing his stricken face, Mum straightened up and dropped Vanessa's foot.

Malcolm put his hands on Mum's shoulders. "Nicola, I'm so sorry. There's been an accident."

Mum's knees gave way and she sank onto the red plastic seat next to Vanessa. She dropped the brown lace-up. "No," she said. "Don't tell me."

"I'm so sorry. Oh God." Malcolm looked over his shoulder. "Where's Tim?"

Mum shut her eyes, and the breath came out of her in short puffs, as if she'd been hit in the chest. "He's selling meat." She swallowed. "Malcolm, what is it?"

Malcolm crouched down and put his hands on Mum's shoulders. "It's . . . Oh God, I am so sorry. It's your little one. . . ."

"Not her," Mum said. Now all the breath fell out of her and the blood drained from her face. "Oh please, God, not the baby." And then in a whisper, "Not my baby, don't tell me. Not shot, please. She's been shot? Is she all right?"

"I'm so sorry," Malcolm said, gripping Mum's shoulders tighter. "I'm so, so sorry.

She's dead."

Mum began shaking all over, "What? They were attacked? She was . . . Was she shot? What happened? An ambush?"

"She . . . We got a phone call from Rena. She drowned."

Mum shook her head, bewildered by the impossibility of this. "No! How? She didn't drown. Who drowned her? No! No!" She stood up and pushed Malcolm. "Please no, please no, please no." And then she walked blindly into the bright sun on Main Street, her whole body convulsing with shock. "No! No! No!"

And yet there was Olivia on the spare bed of the neighbor's house, drowned in the duck pond at Mazonwe because somehow that afternoon at the Viljoen's grocery story we all believed that someone else was keeping an eye on her. Aunty Rena assumed she was with me; I assumed she was with Aunty Rena and there was also Duncan, Rena's fourteen-year-old son with whom Olivia might have wandered off without either of us knowing. And after everything else there was to protect her from — land mines, mortars, abduction, ambush — none of us thought a foot of slimy water behind the store was the greatest danger that could confront the baby.

While I was waiting for Mum, Dad and Vanessa to come back from Umtali, I put purple flowers around Olivia's head. Her curls had dried in crisp ringlets on the white, cotton pillowcase. I heard the neighbors' dogs barking and the sound of our Land Rover pulling into the driveway. Then, in the ensuing horrified hush, I could hear Mum running across the veranda, her shoes urgent down the passage into the spare bedroom. She fell into the room, her whole being attached to the small, perfectly still body on the bed. She sank to her knees and I watched her press her pale lips onto Olivia's blue lips and breathe, her eyes closed, her auburn hair streaked across Olivia's ivory-colored face. It looked as if she were trying to exchange breath with her dead child. "My breath for yours. Take me instead. My breath for yours." And when Olivia's lips did not grow any pinker, Mum sank back on her heels and her chin dropped onto her chest.

Dad came to the door. He picked me up and held me against his shoulder. His face an unseeing mask. "You're so brave," he said. "You must be so brave." Behind him, standing in blank disbelief, I saw Vanessa. Her hands were slack by her side, her eyes open, her face utterly composed except for the two silver lines of tears running down her face. When her eyes caught mine, she shook her head very slightly, almost imperceptibly.

Olivia died in the wet season and we buried her in the tiny, muddy community graveyard in the jungle, beneath the Vumba Mountains, where monkeys smashed through the branches of the old trees and birds nested noisily in the canopy. We marked her grave with a granite stone: OLIVIA JANE FULLER BORN 28 . 8 . 76. DIED 9. 1. 78. DEARLY LOVED DAUGHTER, SISTER. At her funeral, which was held at the house of an Afrikaner family who lived near the graveyard, we sang sad country music about loving and losing and about this being a fine time to leave us and we ate Afrikaner food: fatty lamb, boervors and koeksisters. We grieved in the way of stoical people: tight lipped, moist eyed; the remote death, the little funeral. And we sang some more about hard times and bad times and how there are some pains so deep that they just won't ever heal.

Eleven days after Olivia drowned, the Rhodesian government distributed pamphlets in the Tribal Trust Lands with nine new instructions for black civilians:

1. Human curfew from last light to 12 o'clock daily.
2. Cattle, yoked oxen, goats and sheep curfew from last light to 12 o'clock daily.
3. No vehicles, including bicycles and buses to run either in the Tribal Trust Land or the African Purchase Land.
4. No person will either go on or near any high ground or they will be shot.
5. All dogs to be tied up 24 hours each day or they will be shot.
6. Cattle, sheep and goats, after 12 o'clock, are only to be herded by adults.
7. No juveniles (to the age of 16 years) will be allowed out of the kraal area at any time either day or night, or they will be shot.
8. No schools will be open.
9. All stores and grinding mills will be closed.

But far from containing the growing violence, the new controls only seemed to drive the war deeper underground and strangely further into each of us, as if it had become its own force, murderously separate from mankind, unfettered from its authors, wanton and escaping the conventions that humans have laid out for it in those chastened moments between conflicts.

Now when we drove through Zimunya, the place blew empty, as if ghosted. The minefields echoed with ever more explosions. And every morning, my mother rode her horse alone at the top of the farm, skirting the edge of the Himalayas, her gun carelessly slung across her back (instead of across her belly, the way she used to carry it), as if willing herself to be shot through the heart.

It no longer mattered whether Vanessa and I spoke in Received Pronunciation, or whether we spoke at all. The books Mum had read to us on her bed — hours of Rudyard Kipling, Ernest Thompson Seton, C. S. Lewis, Lewis Carroll, Laura Ingalls Wilder — were gone. In their place was silence. Now when the generator was kicked into life, my mother no longer played for us the vinyl recordings of Chopin nocturnes, Strauss waltzes or Brahms concertos, and meals were no longer interrupted by Mum's toasting our uniqueness, "Here's to us, there're none like us!" Instead, there was the wireless, and the dread news — a civilian airliner shot down by guerilla forces in the southwest of the country, the survivors brutally massacred; an escalation of air raids by Rhodesian forces on guerilla training camps in Zambia and Mozambique; the slaying of foreign missionaries by God only knows whom (each side blamed the other).

And then, on October 17, 1978, Umtali was mortared again in the middle of the night by guerilla forces coming into the country from Mozambique, an event that coincided confusingly with a vehement thunderstorm. At our boarding school we were awoken by our matrons trying to remain calm above the scream of bombs and the roll of thunder, "This is not a drill! This is not a drill!" We were hurried out of our beds and ushered down the fire escapes. Then we were pushed onto the floor in the front hall and mattresses were thrown on top of us with such hurried panic that our chins and elbows hit the cement. "Keep your heads down!" the matrons cried. "Silence! Quiet! Shut up!"

Miss Carr took roll call as if life depended on it and kids yelled their names back at her as if doing so might save them from being blown sky high. "Brown, Ann!" "Coetzee, Jane!" "Dean, Lynn!" "De Kock, Annette!" And there were kids crying for their mothers; people were praying out loud, shouting God's name; and the matrons and teachers telling us to shut up and all the time the whining kaboom of another bomb and then more thunder. But above that overwhelming noise I could still hear the insistently loud voice of my sister from the other end of the makeshift bomb shelter, "Bobo! Bobo! Bobo!" and she didn't let up until I shouted back, "Van, I'm here! It's okay! I'm here, man!"

And then she went quiet under her crowded mattress and I went quiet under mine, but the bombs kept coming from the Mutarandanda Hills above Umtali. I imagined that this was how Vanessa and I would die, apt punishment for allowing Olivia to die first. And I suddenly understood that our aliveness and Olivia's death was why my father had gone silent, and my mother had retreated so far from us that she seemed like a figure at the wrong end of a telescope, familiar but too distant to touch.

Then the attack stopped and against all natural laws we were still alive. The matrons came back through and lifted the mattresses off our heads. The boys doubled up in the junior boys' dormitory and the girls were laid head to toe in the senior boys' dormitory — layers of bodies. A few of us slept, but just before dawn we heard more artillery in the hills and we disentangled ourselves from one another, our legs unwrapping from legs, our intertwined fingers uncurling from fingers. "Take cover!" we yelled. We pushed one another and dove under our beds until Miss Carr came back through. "It's okay. It's okay. Those are *our* boys. They're keeping you safe. Get back in your beds. It's safe, those are *our* mortars." Although from my perspective I suddenly knew two things with complete clarity: that regardless of who is firing them, all mortars sound the same; and that nothing would really ever be okay or safe again.

For the next two days the phone in the hostel rang off the hook, and one student after the other was summoned to the teachers' smoke-filled office to speak to their parents. They returned smugly solemn and tear stained to report that their folks had been sleepless with worry about them. Mum and Dad never did telephone Vanessa and me to see if we were all right. So I thought perhaps they didn't care, that they alone among Chancellor Junior School parents were not sleepless with worry about their children. But Vanessa said, "No, it's not that. We've got to be okay on our own. You've got to be much braver than this, Bobo. They *expect* us to be brave now."

A couple of weeks after the attack we went home for the weekend. Mum gave us both a T-shirt, and we understood it was a treat for not being wimpy (the way we were taken to the secondhand bookstore in Salisbury if we were brave at the dentist). The T-shirt showed a beer bottle in the shape of a grenade.Over it were the words COME TO UMTALI AND GET BOMBED!

"There," Mum said. "That's a joke; isn't it funny? It's a pun. Do you know what a pun is?" And then she looked at her hands and her eyes went very pale, "They asked us not to phone you. They said it would clog up the lines. They said we shouldn't . . ." There was a pause. "You do know you must look after each other." She gave us a shaky, uncertain smile. "You do know that, don't you?"

NICOLA FULLER AND
THE END OF RHODESIA

Bo and Van in front of Victoria Falls. Rhodesia, 1978.

My mother has no patience with questions that begin, "What if." But I spend a great deal of my time circling that insensible eddy. What if we had been thinking straight? What if the setting of our lives had been more ordinary? What if we'd tempered passion with caution? "What-ifs are boring and pointless," Mum says. Because however close to irreparably deep madness my mother had gone in her life, she does not now live in a ruined, regretful, Miss Havisham world and she doesn't wish any of her life away, even the awful, painful, damaging parts. "What-ifs are the worst kind of postmortem," she says. "And I hate postmortems. Much better to face the truth, pull up your socks and get on with whatever comes next."

So the truth is this: it's toward the end of the war (fin de everything) and our collective thinking has been so shaken up by the hallucinatory, seductive violence of it all that we can't see our way even to a safer address somewhere else in Rhodesia, let alone out of the country. In any case, it doesn't occur to us to leave. We see our lives as fraught and exciting, terrible and blessed, wild and ensnaring. We see our lives as Rhodesian, and it's not easy to leave a life as arduously rich and difficult as all that.

In addition, leaving was treason talk, cowardly stuff. Mum makes a fist. "The Fullers aren't wimps," she says. "No, you don't walk away from a country you *say* you love without a fight just because things get rough." So the war escalated and escalated until very few families — rural, urban, black or white — were untouched by it and still we held on.

And then something happened that might have changed everything: my father's father died. It took the English relatives a week before any of them thought to let Dad know. "The funeral is in two days," Uncle Toe told Dad. "Sorry you won't be able to make it." My mother's eyes go pale. "Well, we were only in Rhodesia," she says. "It's not as if we'd fallen off the face of the earth." Within hours of receiving the telephone call, Dad got a cheap airplane ticket to England through Friends of Rhodesia, an organization that helped cash-strapped Rhodesians in emergencies. Then he found an Indian tailor in Umtali who agreed to put a suit together overnight. "Cash customer!" he announced. "I need a first-class suit for a third-class price."

The next morning, Dad arrived in London. He changed into the new suit, hired a car and made it to the church two minutes before his father's funeral was due to begin. "It was a showstopper," Mum says. "Here was Tim back from Africa, sunburned and elegant." As a former colony and now renegade country, Rhodesia made frequent and alarming headlines in the international press: RHODESIA — APARTHEID HEADS

NORTH; RHODESIA FACES ITS FINAL HOUR; THE ARMAGEDDON IS ON. My father must have appeared to his relatives as someone suddenly showing up after being forever lost, dark continent vanished. "It couldn't have shocked them more if Donald had sat up in his casket and ordered a pink gin for the road," Mum says.

Dad took a place near a side door and looked at his fellow mourners. I picture them: Lady Fuller sitting stiffly silent in the front row, very elegant in her weeds (I knew so little of my grandfather's second wife that I can think of her only as the name I have seen in lawyer's letters, frozen in my imagination like a caricature from a Noel Coward play); Uncle Toe looking pale and serious in the pew behind her; in his wake a respectable showing of cousins, a few aunts, an uncle or two; then a row of solid navy types; and at the back my grandfather's pig man.

After the vicar had made obligatory noises, everyone was asked to stand and sing "The Day Thou Gavest, Lord, Is Ended." Then a toppish-brass navy officer took the pulpit and was eloquent on the subject of Captain Connell-Fuller's career (skillfully steering his comments so that they sailed with considerable berth around the sore point of my grandfather's never having achieved the much-desired rank of admiral, or even rear admiral). Then an elderly relative stood up and talked about Donald's fondness for polo; the passion he'd developed in his retirement for raising pigs (the pig man gave an unhappy little wheeze); the time he blew up an oak tree at Douthwaite because it was getting in the way of his golf swing (general chortling). Then the congregation was asked to please stand again for a closing hymn, "Eternal Father, Strong to Save."

After that, the old man's coffin was carried out of the church, lowered into a hole in the ground and then as if the first clod of damp English earth on the wooden lid was a starting gun, the quarrel among his heirs began and didn't let up for a generation and a half, by which time there was almost nothing left over which to fight. My mother closes her eyes and shakes her head, "There were, as you know, let us just say, some . . . problems with the will." But Mum won't elaborate. She flaps the air in front of her face, "Troubled water under the bridge and all that," she says. "No point going on and on about it, is there?"

So our fate was one million per cent Rhodesian and even at this late date, we carried on fighting for Rhodesia as if it were the last place on earth, as if to lose it would be the same as losing ourselves. And life — the life that remained — went on in all its increasingly surreal impossibility. Vanessa and I continued to attend our segregated government school, where we prayed with renewed concentration and intensity at morning assembly for our fathers, our brothers, our boys, our men. Every six weeks Dad continued to disappear up in the Himalayas to fight guerilla forces, returning home exhausted, his right shoulder hunched like a broken wing from the perpetual weight of the FN rifle he carried. And Mum continued with farmwork: checking on the cattle by horseback in the morning; spending the afternoons in the tobacco fields; fretting over a pile of unpaid bills in the evenings.

She grew thin and sinewy, her feet calloused in the nailed strips of old tractor tires she now wore for sandals, her hands blistered and toughened. Whatever soft motherliness she had started out with — that smiling young woman in a gingham dress cradling a Shakespeare-saturated Vanessa on the lawn at Lavender's Corner — was all but worn away. But then, one night in September 1979, Mum suddenly shoved herself back from the dining room table, a hand over her mouth, her eyes glassy with nausea. She glared at her plate, "Oh, the smell!" she said. Knowing the telltale signs, my father put down his knife and fork. "All right, Tub?"

Mum held up a finger, "I'll be fine."

She hurried from the room and Dad watched her retreating back. Then he pushed away his plate, lit a cigarette and put his head in his hands — the smoke curled up through his thinning hair. Outside, insects continued to pulse; Mum's dairy cows screamed at a disturbance (a stray dog perhaps) and up in the hills there was a muffled explosion — something or someone on the cordon sanitaire detonating a mine. Whether she was ready for it or not, motherhood had imposed itself on Mum once again.

It is an ancient and misguided ruse, this introduction of a baby to trick the universe back into innocence, an effort to force the unraveling world to meet the comforting routine of a milk-scented nursery, a wish to have our sins washed clean by the blamelessness inherent in a newborn. But by late 1979, our country was beyond the reach of any child, however miraculous. The war had gone on so long and had become so desperate that it wasn't a civil war anymore so much as it was a civilians' war, a hand-to-hand, deeply personal conflict. The front line had spread from the borders to the urban areas to our doorsteps, and if we didn't all have bloody hands, we were all related by blood to someone who did.

And now, awfully, the half-life of our violence had been extended indefinitely: the war had turned biological. Rhodesian Special Forces with the help of South African military had salted the water along the Mozambique border with cholera and warfarin; they had injected tins of food with thallium and dropped them into conflict zones; they had infused clothes with organophosphate and left them out for the guerilla fighters and for sympathizers of the guerilla cause. And they had planted anthrax in the villages; and more than ten thousand men, women and children living in the country's Tribal Trust Lands were sickened with sometimes fatal necrotic boils, fevers, shock and respiratory failure in what would end up being the largest outbreak of anthrax among humans in recorded history.

All of this ongoing and deepening enmity, even as the leaders of the Rhodesian government and the leaders of the liberation forces were meeting at Lancaster House in London to discuss how to transition from rogue state to majority rule — from war to peace. Lord Carrington, British secretary of state for foreign and commonwealth affairs, opened the meeting tersely. "It is, I must say, a matter of great regret and disappointment to me and my colleagues that hostilities are continuing during this conference. . . ."

There had been peace talks before — held in the carriage of a train on the railway bridge across the Victoria Falls in 1975, for example — but the dialogue had always broken down. So it was something of a surprise — actually, to some it was an irredeemable blow — when on December 6, 1979, after three months of brittle negotiations, the Lancaster House Agreement was finally signed by all the relevant leaders. And just like that, it was settled. The war was over. Within a matter of weeks, the country would have a new name, Zimbabwe. And we would have a new prime minister, Robert Mugabe.

At school we were told that from now on, we were all equal. After morning announcements, we no longer sang "Onward Christian Soldiers" at assembly; now we sang "Precious Lord, Take My Hand," which put our relationship to God in a whole new light, bordering on an erstwhile frowned-upon Public Display of Affection (until now, it would not have occurred to us to ask even our own parents to take our hands, let alone the Lord). And instead of praying for our boys, our brothers, our fathers, our men, we now prayed for peace, unity and forgiveness. Instead of mashed potatoes for lunch, we were now served sadza and we were encouraged to eat it the traditional way: rolled into balls in the palm of one hand and eaten with fingers. Our new black matron (much younger and more energetic than our old white one) told us that changing the words we used would be the beginning of changing our hearts. She told us that we should say *liberation fighters* instead of *terrs;* we should say *indigenous people* instead of *munts;* we should not call grown men "garden boys" or "boss boys" — we should call them "gardeners" or "headmen."

"I suppose we all saw it coming," Mum says, "but it was still a terrible shock to lose the war like that, lose the country, lose everything. One morning we woke up and it had all been decided and there was nothing left to fight for." She leans back in her chair, her mouth folded at the edges as if the memory of this time exhausts her. "Everyone was going on and on about peace and reconciliation, but I knew it wasn't going to work like that. No, I knew it wasn't going to be simple and easy."

Zimbabwean refugees who had spent the

war in Mozambique came flooding back over the border and began squatting along the river at the top of Robandi, silting up the farm's water supply and bringing tick disease into our cattle herds with their undipped livestock. "So we ended up with a whole new fight on our hands," Mum says. "I wanted those squatters off our farm. They wouldn't leave. We were harassed and exhausted; our nerves were in shreds." Mum found herself unable to sleep, jumpy and tearful. "I suppose now we would say I had depression, but in those days we didn't have a word for it." (Actually, we did. Vanessa and I would have said Mum was having "a wobbly.")

In light of this, Dad decided it would be best for everyone if we left Robandi, left the squatters, left the apricot-peach colored house and its constant reminders of everything we'd lost. He signed a year-long contract as section manager on Devuli Ranch, a vast, remote piece of nearly wild earth in the southeast of the country. His job was to round up the cattle that had gone feral over the seven-hundred-and-fifty-thousand-acre ranch during the course of the war. "A year away from it all," Dad says. "Some real peace, a chance to breathe for a bit."

Once a fortnight for the next year Dad packed a mosquito net, a sleeping bag, two bottles of brandy, a tin of coffee, some rice and a gun. Then he set up camp in the wild, unpeopled mopane woodlands far from any sign of civilization. At night he slept under a darkly innocent sky, a day's full drive on rough bush tracks from the nearest human habitation. And I have no proof that day after day he walked six years of fighting out of his system, but it seems as likely an explanation as any for how he recovered most of the pieces of himself after that bush war.

To begin with, he brought Mum with him to camp. He set her up for the day on a camp chair in the shelter of a baobab tree with his best pair of binoculars and a new bird book. Then he went off to track and capture cattle. Once a week, he shot a young impala ram and hung it to cure in a wire safe so that there would always be fresh meat for her. He maintained a burning fire all night and he lit paraffin lamps around the camp so that she wouldn't trip or stand on a snake if she needed to get up in the night.

But Mum didn't respond to the isolation as well as Dad hoped. She looked haunted and confused. She couldn't concentrate long enough to read a single page of her book and, distressingly, she lost all interest in the birds. Her skin grew yellow as if the intense, low-veldt sun was stealing her color, and she began to have heart palpitations. Doctor Mitchell was alarmed. He ordered my mother into the hospital. "Bed rest until this child is born," he insisted. So Mum left the ranch and stayed in the hospital in Umtali until the baby, a boy, arrived via Cesarean section in late June 1980.

"He had the bluest eyes you've ever seen, just like Dad's," Mum says. "He looked perfect — perfect little face, perfect little body." She puts her fingers to her lips. "But there was something not right inside; the back of his palate, you know, wasn't quite formed. . . ." Still, the baby managed to nurse a little and when he cried, Mum held him on her shoulder and sang to him. But as the days went by, the baby became more lethargic, he seemed less able to grip Mum's fingers and his crying turned plaintive. "We were waiting for a medical device from South Africa," Mum says. "Something to attach to his palate so that he could swallow without choking." But before the shipment could arrive from Johannesburg, one of the nurses came to Mum's bed. "You'd better go and see your child," the nurse said. "He isn't well."

Mum held the stitches across the bottom of her stomach and hurried out of the maternity ward into the nursery. "Lots of the nurses were black by then," Mum says, "and after everything we'd been through . . . well, I suppose it's only natural. They weren't very sympathetic." Mum sighs. "They might even have been a little vindictive." She looks away. "Anyway, it was very cruel." When she got to the nursery, Mum found the baby jarringly still in his crib. "Oh God, it was just awful," Mum says. "He died alone. You know? He died all alone, the little thing." She scooped up her son's tiny, stiff body and rocked him — "I'm sorry," she told him, "Oh, I am so, so sorry" — letting her tears fall on his face. Then she carefully put the baby back in the hospital crib, covered him with a blanket and went to her knees.

She waited for the old, customary pain to overwhelm her. Instead, everything Mum had ever felt receded and receded until she could hardly comprehend her own physical self anymore: her knees on the red cement floor had self-defensively deadened against any more pain; her recent incision was nothing more than a remote pang. Nothing, nothing — a void. My parents never named the child. Mum shakes her head. "He didn't live long enough. We just wanted to try to forget, move on." But unable to imagine a brother without a name, Vanessa and I privately christened the absent baby Richard.

He is, of my three dead siblings, the most unmentioned and the most unmentionable.

For weeks after the baby had been born and died, Mum lay in the lacy-hot shade of a camel thorn tree near the ranch house at Devuli, radiant with emptiness. At night, when the generator was turned on for a few hours of electricity, she drank brandy and played and replayed "The Final Farewell" from a Roger Whittaker album. Sometimes in the cooler mornings she rode her horse along the dry riverbank that ran along the boundary of the ranch and she hummed that song to herself and she thought how she had no fear of death and about how she did not have words for how she loved the child she had lost. No words at all.

More than twenty years after we had given up Robandi, I returned to the Burma Valley in October 2002 to see what traces of my family remained there. We didn't live on Robandi for very long — a little more than half a dozen years — not even a seventh of Mum's life, as I write this. But those years have blossomed like a stain over everything else in her life because of what we lost there. Even now, Robandi is the geography of my nightmares: the rusty streaks on the walls of the white barns where the roofs had oxidized; the sour-breath smell of the work-shops; the toughening astringent of gun oil against fingers. If I peel back the corner of memories of that place, what races in is too big for me to feel at one sitting — no mere piece of land can be responsible for that.

I found the essential shape of our old farm unchanged, although it was no longer recognizable as the struggling commercial enterprise my parents ran during the war. The avenue of flamboyant trees still ran from the Mazonwe road up to the apricot-peach colored house, but the road had washed away. The fences had collapsed and instead of crops or cattle, scrubby bush had begun to encroach. Where Mum had kept a neat, thatched dairy, there was only a tangle of lantana thicket. I drove as far as I could on a new, improvised trail that bumped over old contours in what was once a tobacco field. Finally I left the car by the culvert where the cobra used to live and walked up to the house.

There were no recent tracks on the road, and when I reached it, the house appeared abandoned, its windows broken, sections of asbestos sheeting missing from the roof and gray patches of mold spreading over the apricot-peach walls. The garden had dried up and died. I knocked at the front door (still engrained with scratches from the long-ago claws of all our dogs) and a young man came to the door. He was shirtless in the October heat and looked as if he had just woken up. I apologized for the intrusion, introduced myself and asked him if I might sit on the veranda for a moment to look at the view.

The young man considered my request for a while, then he shrugged and said the view did not belong to him. "Look at it if you want," he said. But before I could thank him, he shut the door and I was left alone. So I sat on the veranda and looked at that deadly, beautiful view over Robandi — the red-dusted boulders, the blue-gray kopjes, the bush-smoked Himalayas — across the valley to John Parodi's Italian-inspired farm with its avenues of Mediterranean cypresses, its Ionic columns and its brick-paved court-yard.

In retrospect, of course, everyone should have anticipated this outcome. We should have seen that a story begun with such one-sided, unconscious joviality — jewel-colored liqueurs and Portuguese wine on a rain-washed Rhodesian October morning — would end less than a decade later in defeat and heartbreak. But in the glow of love, in the heat of battle, in the cushioned denial of the present, how few have the wisdom to look forward with unclouded hindsight. Not my parents, certainly. Not most of us. But most of us also don't pay so dearly for our prejudices, our passions, our mistakes. Lots of places, you can harbor the most ridiculous, the most ruining, the most intolerant beliefs and be hurt by nothing more than your own thoughts.

I had just turned fourteen during the Easter holidays of 1983 when Mum broke the news to me that John Parodi had been shot to death on his own veranda by an assassin or assassins unknown, the war bleeding retribution and carnage long after its official end. The people who found his body said that John's staining handprint ran the length of the veranda as he tried to reach his son, Giovanni. And Giovanni himself — only fourteen but already handsome in that eyebrow-winged way of his thick-shouldered father and with his mother's irreverently laughing mouth — had been abducted from the farm by his father's killers. Madeline, John's eighteen-year-old daughter was not at home on the day of the attack but for months and years after her father's funeral, she rode a motorbike through the Himalayas, searching for signs of her brother, calling his name profitlessly into the hot, purple hills, "Giovanni! Giovanni!"

No one starts a war warning that those involved will lose their innocence — that children will definitely die and be forever lost as a result of the conflict; that the war will not end for generations and generations, even after cease-fires have been declared and peace treaties have been signed. No one starts a war that way, but they should. It would at least be fair warning and an honest admission: even a good war — if there is such a thing — will kill anyone old enough to die.

PART THREE

Power said to the world, "You are mine."
The world kept it prisoner on her throne.
Love said to the world, "I am thine."
The world gave it the freedom of her house.

— RABINDRANATH TAGORE

I always keep a supply of stimulant handy in
case I see a snake, which I also keep handy.

— W. C. FIELDS

NICOLA FULLER OF CENTRAL AFRICA AND THE TREE OF FORGETFULNESS

Mum at her fish ponds. Zambia, 2008.

If I had to put a date on the moment Mum began to swim away from us, I would say it was after Richard died, because for years after that she was like someone whose refuge was a remote subaqua world. And how could she have been otherwise? Mum's brain, already highly strung with a genetic predisposition to "funny moods, depression, mental wobbliness" must certainly have tripped on

301

the tragedy and stress of what she had lost: three children, a war, a farm. To say nothing of what she had lost of herself: the whimsical Kenyan girl, the winklepicker-wearing bride, the hilarious-amount-of-fun young mother.

And although sometimes in the years after the baby's death, Mum would come to the surface of her subaqua refuge, occasionally for months and months at a time, the threat that she'd recede from us again was always there. Something would set her off — a minor upset (the car breaking down) or a major blow (her mother's death in 1993) — and she would be back below our reach, sleeping late into the morning, unconcerned about her appearance, listlessly incurious about the world around her.

And then — alarmingly — something altogether different began to happen: as well as sinking into subaqua depths, Mum would now sometimes seem to lose her tether altogether and float sky high. On these occasions she would be riddled with energy: riding her horse with wild indifference as opposed to wild courage; driving at high speeds on rough roads; drinking with no care and less joy. A couple of car wrecks date back to this time: spinning the vehicle elegantly on the apex of its left front headlight; an abrupt sideways flip into a storm drain. "Bloody silly place to put a ditch," a sympathetic neighbor said, pulling her to safety.

Then in 1998, eighteen years after Richard had come and gone and five years after the death of her mother, Mum had the worst episode of madness ever. Her father had died earlier in the year, peacefully drifting off after his evening allowance of J & B at the age of nearly ninety, beloved of everyone in the nursing home near Perth, Scotland, in which he spent his final days. Mum took his death as well as could be expected and the funeral at Waternish went off without a hitch. "Skye people are very respectful of the dead," Mum says approvingly. "So we didn't have to pay the toll to go over the bridge from the mainland. Wasn't that nice?"

Dad led the procession to the Trumpan Church, followed by the vicar, followed by the hearse, followed by Auntie Glug and Uncle Sandy. Dad, accustomed to covering long distances on rough African roads, kept up a decent pace, weaving expertly around the baleful sheep as if they were potholes. "The vicar was flicking his head-lights at us like mad because he wanted us to slow down, but Dad thought it meant we should go faster. I think it's the only time a hearse has gone whizzing through Skye on two wheels."

The little funeral procession, slightly breathless from what had felt to most of them like a rally-car race, gathered around the grave next to the ruined church. Uncle Sandy — properly kitted out in kilt, Glengarry bonnet and sporran — began to play "Flowers of the Forest" on his bagpipes. "And suddenly, right in the middle of it, with the bagpipes going and all of us softly weeping, the clouds parted and a brilliant sky opened up overhead. Then a figure appeared just beyond the church wall in a blue anorak. We all saw him." Mum's eyes go Clanranald fey. "And we all agreed it was the ghost of dear, shell-shocked Uncle Allan come to welcome my father to the other side. A *very* Highland greeting I should have said."

But in spite of the successful funeral and before Mum left Scotland, there were signs that she was about to throw a wobbly. Her eyes went light yellow and she began to counsel anyone who would listen on the best way for the Scots to plot their secession from England. ("You should try UDI, like we had in Rhodesia.") Finally, she packed pounds and pounds of haggis in her suitcase, which she then tried to smuggle through international customs.

When she got back to Zambia, Mum didn't sleep or eat, whirring around their tiny borrowed cottage near Lusaka like a trapped hummingbird. She gave up the usual niceties — tea before breakfast, the dogs' evening walk, a soak in the bathtub before supper with the BBC World Service — and skipped directly to a steady infusion of Valium and brandy, which didn't seem to have even a remotely sedating effect on her. Dad, who had managed Mum's previous wobblies by ignoring them, was genuinely worried by this one. All the hours he could spare, he sat outside her bedroom door smoking cigarettes and playing solitaire. Inside, Mum lay in a state of pretend sleep, plotting her escape to remote and impossible places: the Democratic Republic of Congo ("Je m'appelle Nicola Fuller de Afrique centrale!") or London's West End (*Starlight Express, Cats, Les Misérables!*). And the moment she sensed Dad's vigil had lapsed, she bolted, driving into Lusaka to buy airplane tickets to London or making it as far as Lubumbashi before being retrieved by my father. ("Oh, why must everyone *bully* me so much?")

This went on for a few months until finally, ragged with exhaustion, asthmatic and underweight, she admitted herself to a clinic in Lusaka, banging on the gates in the middle of the night, barefoot and trembling, having run miles on a dirt road, until a watchman heard her and let her in. The next day Dad drove Mum five or six hours across the border to the psychiatric ward of a Zimbabwean hospital. There she was strapped to a bed and drugged to a standstill until she could be stabilized, diagnosed, medicated. "My mad pills, my happy pills, my panic pills, my sleeping pills," she says. "Wonderful psychiatrist I had, *very* talented. He knew exactly what was wrong with me and he knew what to give me to fix it." Mum jabs her walking stick in the ground a few times for emphasis. "It was just a little chemical imbalance."

We're having this conversation on a late-afternoon walk back from the Zambezi River to the Tree of Forgetfulness. The dogs surge ahead of us, rooting out snake smells and scaring up locusts the size of small pigeons. "So yes," Mum agrees, "I am mad. We *all* know that, but it's not a problem. It's nothing Cairo Chemist can't put right." Suddenly she puts her binoculars to her eyes with a little gasp of excitement and says, "Look, a paradise flycatcher. How wonderful! What a glorious tail! Did you see it?" But she doesn't offer me her binoculars. "Off he goes. There, look at him — swoop, swoop." Mum inhales deeply, a soft smile on her lips.

"Ah, I love the evenings," she says. "Such a reward after the daily toil, isn't it?"

And she's right. The evenings here on the north bank of the Zambezi River are tremulously beautiful. A shaky ribbon of blue smoke from a nearby village's cooking fire hangs over the farm. Emerald-spotted doves are calling, "My mother is dead, my father is dead, my relatives are dead and my heart goes dum-dum-dum." Frogs are bellowing from the causeway. The air boils with beetles and cicadas, mosquitoes and tsetse flies. Egrets, white against the gray-pink sky are floating upriver to roost in the winterthorn trees in the middle of Dad's bananas. "I won't let him chop down those trees," Mum says, "the birds love them."

But you can't have all this life on one end without a corresponding amount of death and decay on the other: in the morning, my parents' maid, Hilda Tembo ("Big H" to the family), will sweep up half a bucket of insect carcasses and two gecko bodies from under the Tree of Forgetfulness. Months from now three of the Jack Russells will have been killed by a cobra in Dad's office, and one will have been eaten by a crocodile in Mum's fish ponds. And Dad will walk out of the bedroom one morning to see a python coiled in cartoonish perfection around Wallace (the late cat). "You learn not to mourn every little thing out here," Mum says. She shakes her head. "No, you can't, or you'd never, ever stop grieving."

What my mother won't say — lost in all her talk of chemicals and pills — is that she knows not only the route grief takes through blood but also the route it takes through the heart's cracks. What she won't tell me is that recovering from the madness of grief wasn't just a matter of prescriptions, but of will-power. "I sometimes used to envy the people you see running up and down the Kafue Road in hessian sacks," she said once. And it is true that Mum seriously considered that level of deep, irretrievable insanity an option. But instead, she took a different route and she regained herself and that had very little to do with the *very* talented psychiatrist and everything to do with forgiveness: she forgave the world and her mind returned. She gave herself amnesty and her soul had a home again. The forgiveness took years and it took this farm and it took the Tree of Forgetfulness. It took all of that, but above all it took the one thing grief could never steal from my mother: her courage.

For nearly a year after Mum had been strapped down in the mental ward of the hospital in Zimbabwe and given various doses of mad pills, happy pills, panic pills and sleeping pills, she stayed in bed in the little borrowed cottage outside Lusaka, utterly exhausted. By now Vanessa and I were both married with young children of our own (I in America, and Vanessa, for the time being, in England), and neither of us could easily come home. So Dad fussed around Mum; brought her tea; took the dogs out for their evening walk so they would leave her in peace; ran her a bath each evening and tuned her radio to the BBC World Service. But in her midfifties, it would seem Mum had finally given up.

She took the pills prescribed to her by the *very* talented psychiatrist and drew the curtains. A bat took up residence in her closet and ruined her Royal Ascot hats and Mum did not go to war with it; charcoal burners came onto the place and their axes sang against old-growth mukwa trees and she did not go to war with them; thieves took off with her old treadle sewing machine (the device responsible for helping my mother create our infamously tortuous Fancy Dress costumes) and she just sighed.

Dad tried everything. "I think I saw an oribi this evening when I was out with the dogs," he would say (a sighting usually guaranteed to make Mum leap to her feet, binoculars in hand). Or he'd bring Mum piri piri prawns and proper wine (in a bottle as opposed to a box) from the Italian merchant in Lusaka, but she would retire after a single prawn and half a glass of wine. And even when Dad brought home a new puppy, a comical, smoke-colored Great Dane cross Labrador ("the best halves of both," Dad promised), Mum could manage little more than a wan smile of thanks.

So at night while Mum slept, Dad built a campfire outside their little cottage; he propped up his chin on a thumb, two fingers nestled around a cigarette on his bottom lip and he worried his way to a solution. "There was no question of letting her give up," Dad says. "No, I knew all she needed was a little encouragement and she'd be all right." Dad pauses and rubs his fist under each eye. When he continues, his voice is thicker. "She never gave up on me through everything," he says. "No, as far as I am concerned, she has always been the most number one lady in all of Africa."

After we'd left Robandi, my father said he would never again try to own an African farm. "You put your blood and sweat into a place and then . . ." Dad shook his head.

"The government goes apex over teakettle — there's a coup, squatters show up, or the wind changes direction — and suddenly it's all gone. No, there's no point; you can still work in Africa without trying to own any of it." And then Dad quoted Marcus Garvey, "Africa is for the Africans."

So to begin with, Dad took a position as manager of a massive tobacco estate in Malawi. His boss was Malawi's president for life, the aging dictator Hastings Kamuzu Banda, or His Excellency as he preferred to be called (H.E. for short). It was, Mum says, a useful and humbling experience to have a very powerful, very serious black boss after the white supremacy of Rhodesia. "A short, sharp education on how to live and behave in a black African country *run* by black Africans," she says.

H.E.'s actual date of birth was an official state secret, but he was undeniably old and unquestionably old-fashioned. He affected crisply tailored three-piece suits with matching handkerchiefs and went everywhere with a traditional fly whisk, as if expecting perpetual annoyance. "Everyone was scared stiff of him," Mum says. "You had to bow and scrape and be at his beck and call. And if you upset him, then that was it." Her eyes open wide. "The end of our first year on the estate, the deputy president of our company had some little disagreement with H.E., and the next thing we knew, his Mercedes had gone over a cliff, mysteriously riddled with bullet holes."

Days after my parents' arrival in the country, an official spy was sent to the tobacco estate to keep an eye on their activities, and to ensure that they were behaving in an acceptably Malawian manner at all times: no long hair or beards for men; women had to wear skirts below the knee (no trousers allowed); no kissing in public; no uncensored literature; and above all, H.E. was to be constantly revered and honored. "You weren't even allowed to throw away or burn a newspaper if it contained his image," Mum says, "which got tricky because every edition of the *Malawian Times,* or whatever it was, had lots of photographs of him in it — hovering over this hospital bed, blessing that school-child, getting out of another bullet-proof helicopter. In the end, it was safest not to buy a newspaper at all, because where would you store them all?"

Mum and Dad's letters were steamed open and all their phone calls were monitored by a spy working at the telephone exchange. "You could hear the spy eating his lunch over the line," Mum says. "Nshima and relish.

Squelch-squelch." And once or twice Dad was dragged off by the police for questioning. "Pages and pages of accusations of all the stuff we were supposed to have been up to," Mum says. She takes a sip of tea and absentmindedly picks a tick off one of the Jack Russells sitting on her lap. "Oh yes, things could get very sinister in a hurry and it was very stressful," she says. "I got a plague of boils, Dad's hair started to fall out, we both had malaria all the time. When our two-year contract was up, we had had enough of that. Two years was all we could take."

So my parents found work in Zambia with a German company, raising maize, soya beans, tobacco and cattle on a farm near the Zaire border. "We liked working for zee Germans," Mum says. She puts the Jack Russell nose to nose against her face. "Didn't we, Bumble Bee? Yes, we loved zee Germans." Mum gives me a look. "Well, you know what Germans are like. They preferred things orderly and picturesque when they came out for their annual visit. So they bought us a couple of bush horses to graze nicely in the home paddock and they got us a set of new wineglasses, all matching instead of just whatever wasn't broken. And they imported terrifying chemicals to keep the pool blue so they could go for invigorating swims or whatever it is Germans like to do before breakfast."

Mum brought a Chinyanja phrasebook and dictionary and began to practice on Adamson Phiri, the cook. "Muli bwanji. Dzina landa ndine Nicola Fuller of Central Africa," she said. She especially liked the Chinyanja word for brain. "Bongo," she said triumphantly, "bongo, bongo. Isn't that onomatopoeic? That describes my brain perfectly." Then she pulled out her Berlitz German course left over from the days Dad worked for the veterinary-supply company in Kenya ("I knew this would come in handy one day," she said, triumphantly) and walked around the house asking the animals, "Wie geht es dir?"

And for a few years, Mum and Dad were, on the whole, very happy. It is true that some of their Mkushi farming neighbors were armed and excitable — "all those Yugoslavs and Greeks," Mum says appreciatively, "very volatile" — but at least there wasn't a war on. And the Zambian bush ponies were stubborn and they reared, but they gave Mum the idea that she would like to show-jump again, so she bought herself a proper horse (a Hanoverian called Hannah) and began to enter agricultural shows. And Dad, inspired by Mum's show-jumping, took up polo again, competing in dusty, dangerous tournaments in Lusaka. ("Gangway! Gangway!" riders would shriek as yet another out-of-control amateur bolted screaming toward the goal.)

But then something happened halfway around the world that changed everything. In late 1989, the Berlin Wall came down and almost overnight, the predictable Cold War system on which Zambia (a socialist country) had relied for so long was far less certain. The markets opened up, currency controls started to collapse, American food aid poured into the country and suddenly farmers couldn't sell their maize and soya beans locally for any price at all. "Why buy food when it's being given to you for nothing?" Dad says.

By the early 1990s, the Germans were getting anxious. "They wanted to get their money out of Zambia," Mum says. So the farm was sold and my parents found themselves without work and without a place to live. A friend offered them the use of Oribi Ridge, a little cottage with adjoining stables and an orange orchard on a hilly, msasa-forested plot twenty miles or so east of Lusaka. "Rent free," Mum says, shaking her head in amazement. "Isn't that kind? We've been so lucky with our friends all our lives. The only thing Graeme asked us to do in exchange was to stop the villagers around there chopping down his trees — all virgin forest you know, very wonderful, very old miombo woodland."

So Mum and Dad moved into a tiny cottage on Oribi Ridge with half a dozen ponies, several dogs, Mum's books, the hunting prints, the bronze of Wellington, and the Le Creuset pots. But even with her horses and her dogs, Mum was bored and restless. For most of the last twenty-five years, she had helped my father run a series of farms, and now, without the routine of the seasons, without the discipline of seedbeds and without the rigor of grading sheds, Mum's inclination to be either subaqua, or cut afloat from the world, was more easily indulged.

For his part, without a farm to run, Dad did the only thing he could think of for work: he traded fish in Lusaka out of the back of a small truck. Trader Tim, Mum called him, and although she kept her voice light, there was a disparaging edge to the comment. Dad looked a little bewildered, as if his feet missed the pacing of earth. He complained of feeling out of shape and liverish, and he gave up eating breakfast. "It's a farmer's meal," he explained, "and I am not a farmer anymore." But still he couldn't help himself, absentmindedly picking up and sniffing the soil wherever he stood; mentally calculating its probable pH; subconsciously assessing its appropriateness for tobacco, soya beans or maize; automatically feeling its ability to hold moisture.

And so one Sunday morning in 1995, Dad set out from the cottage and followed a poachers' route off Oribi Ridge to the edge of the escarpment overlooking the Zambezi River and he sat out there until sunset, smoking and thinking and scribbling figures on the back of a cigarette packet. Dad can't say exactly what resolved in his head that day, or why, but when he came back to the cottage that night, he told Mum he had a plan. "Why trade fish when you can grow them yourself?" he asked. "We're going to get a piece of land on the river, and we're going to start farming fish."

Mum looked up from the campfire. "But I thought you said Africa was for the Africans," she said.

Dad squatted in front of the campfire and turned a log until a flame shook awake from the embers. "I did," he said. He lit a cigarette with the glowing end of the log and squinted through the smoke at Mum. "I did."

The next week, Dad drove two hours to the banks of the middle Zambezi River and presented himself at the boma of Chief Sikongo. He took off his hat, handed a gift to the chief's assistant (a bag of maize meal and some cooking oil) and asked if he could have an audience with the chief. He was told to wait under a mango tree. So Dad settled himself down in the shade and passed the time watching the villagers come and go from the river while chickens pecked around his feet and dogs curled up next to him in dusty nests. A few hours later, the chief emerged from his palace (a modest brick house), and after the customary back-and-forth (How are the rains in Lusaka? How was the journey?), my father explained to the chief that he wanted a small farm on the edge of the river on which to raise fish in ponds, bananas in a field, a few sheep here and there. The chief listened and then told Dad to come back in one week with a pair of size six Bata slip-ons. ("That shouldn't be too difficult," Dad thought.)

So the next week Dad returned to Chief Sikongo's boma with a pair of size six Bata slip-ons. Again he handed the gift to the chief's assistant and waited for an audience with the chief under the mango tree in the liquid-white Zambezi sun. A few hours later, the chief appeared, and again Dad explained his need for a farm — the fish, the bananas, the sheep. The chief listened and then he told Dad to return in one month with a portable radio, spare batteries and some salt.

So in a month Dad returned to the chief's boma with the gifts, as instructed. And yet again he explained how his farm would work and how many of the chief's subjects he would employ — people to work on the fish section, people to work on the bananas, shepherds for the sheep. The chief listened and nodded and occasionally muttered something to his assistant. And then he told Dad to come back in two months, this time with a dinner jacket and a bullock.

So like some character in a fairy story on an ever more impossible quest, Dad returned to the chief again and again with offerings, with explanations and with calculations. Eighteen times he went back to the boma and waited under the mango tree, usually all through the burning middle of the day, for the chief to see him. Eighteen times the chief accepted Dad's gifts and heard his story and at the end of eighteen times, Dad finally said, "Chief Sikongo, it's not just for me alone. Your subjects will be trained to farm fish, they will have proper housing and there will be jobs for women. All of us together will make something of this place." Dad stood one legged, schoolboylike, and scratched his calf with the toe of his shoe. "Pamodzi, pamodzi."

The chief looked up at Dad and he nodded. "All right, I have seen," he said. There was a pause and then the chief opened his hands and pointed downstream. "There is one piece of land you can have below the bridge; no one is using it — there is no road, there are no buildings. I think it will work for your scheme."

Dad blinked at the chief, almost not daring to believe it. Then he remembered himself and gave a little bow. "Zikomo kwambili, Chief Sikongo," he said.

So Dad's proposal for the fish and banana farm was put before the Siavonga District Counsil (a month or two passed). Then the land was inspected by a local counsilor and was approved for development (another few months went by). Then a planning officer went to Zimbabwe to see for himself what a fish farm might look like, and after a delay of yet more months, he approved the project. Then the land was surveyed and surveyed again. And all of this happened in accordance with the weather; the availability of transportation; the health of various officials (malaria so often striking at an inopportune time). So that nearly three years after his first meeting with the chief, Dad still did not have title to the farm.

Meantime, Mum had had her two million percent nervous breakdown and now she lay in her bed in the borrowed cottage at Oribi Ridge, the curtains closed against the light, her mind shut against the world, her Royal Ascot hats in ruins. She sold her horses, she gave up reading, she no longer walked the dogs. Dad fretted around her, trying to cajole her out of bed and at night he sat alone by the campfire, kicking the night's embers into life and staring into the flames, thinking and considering that perhaps his instincts had been correct in the first place; perhaps it was folly to try to own land in Africa again.

Then all of a sudden, just as he was about to give up hope, all the pieces of ritual and custom and law shook loose and resolved themselves on a land officer's desk into an acceptable application. And one morning in February 1999, a few weeks before my father's fifty-ninth birthday, the Land Office of Zambia issued him title deed, a ninety-nine-year lease, for a small farm in the middle Zambezi Valley. Dad raced home and burst into the bedroom. "Tub!" he shouted. "A farm! We've got ourselves a farm!" Mum turned toward the door, lowered the blankets and sat up. "What?" she asked.

"A farm," Dad said again, "on the banks of the Zambezi River." Dad waggled his hips. "How about some plonk in the garden?" He held up a box of South African wine. "Come on, Tub!" And he put an arm under Mum's shoulder and got her out of bed. Flustered and a bit shaky, Mum put her hands to her hair and tried to flatten it. "It's okay," Dad said, calming down a little. "Take your time. I'll wait for you outside."

Dad went into the garden, the dogs spilling after him, and he poured a little wine into two glasses. Several minutes passed, and then he heard the bedroom door open. The dogs sprang to their feet, their tails beating a fervent greeting. Even in the steamy February heat, Mum was dressed as if she were preparing for a long, difficult journey to a lonely, cold place — pajamas, a shawl around her neck, thick socks — but she had brushed her hair as best she could (it still skewed sideways) and there was a line of bright lipstick on her lips.

"There you are, Tub," Dad said.

Mum sat down next to Dad and looked out at the msasa forest. "Hm," she said.

"Here," Dad said, handing her a glass.

Mum raised her glass. "Here's to us," she said. She smiled. "There's none like us, and if there were, they're all dead."

Dad took a sip of his wine. "You can say that again," he said.

My father bought two working donkeys from the Zambian Ministry of Agriculture. His old cattle manager from Mkushi who had gone on to be Mum's groom insisted on coming down to the farm to work with the donkeys. "If you have some donkeys," Dama Zulu told my father, "then I must come and help you." Mr. Zulu appraised the donkeys with his expert eye, "We can call them Flash and Lightning," he concluded with what turned out to be prescient optimism. And so my father and Mr. Zulu, the donkeys and a span of men from the surrounding villages worked together for months. They cleared the farm's boundary, pulled stumps, created firebreaks, opened up thick scrub. It was terrifically hot — far too hot to sleep in a tent ("You'd roast to death," Dad says) — so Dad and Mr. Zulu slept under a tarpaulin strung across some mopane branches. And as people do who are so closely thrown together, they began to acquire one another's habits: Mr. Zulu, for example, taking on something of my father's bandy-legged walk and his manner of not speaking except in short barks; and my father settling into Mr. Zulu's habit of walking everywhere with

323

a long stick, a defense against snakes and ropey vines of buffalo bean. "And at night they both got bitten to death by mosquitoes," Mum adds. "Mosquitoes like jackals, siphoning out gallons of blood until there was nothing left of Dad or Mr. Zulu except little bits of skin."

"Oh, you do exaggerate, Tub," Dad says.

"Well, she can put that in one of her Awful Books then," Mum replies.

By April, Mr. Zulu, whose two obsessions were land and wives, had damaged two young women from the village (and had married one of them, much to the consternation of his first three wives) and Dad had malaria, but a road had been cleared to the river and it was possible now to see the layout of the farm; the top mud flats where the fish ponds would go; the more loamy soil below where the bananas would fit; a stretch by the river reserved for a future fishing lodge and bar. "Today," Dad told Mr. Zulu, "I am going to get the madam from Lusaka so she can choose a place to put her hut. You must also choose where you want to live."

Mr. Zulu staked his claim on a small hill where he would be lord and master of all he surveyed and could see any unsuspecting, promising young woman coming from a mile off. Meanwhile, my mother made her way to a tree slightly tucked away at the sloping edge of Mr. Zulu's hill. It was a tree of modest height, with a rounded spreading crown of leathery dark leaves and drooping branches. She thumped her walking stick on the ground under the tree. "Here," she said. She stared up into the tree's branches, "so full of birds," and announced, "I want my house right here."

Mr. Zulu came down from his hill and stood with my mother under the tree. He lit a cigarette and stared up at the tree's canopy. Then he reached up and pulled at the leaves. "Do you know what this tree is?" he asked.

My mother frowned. "Maybe a false marula?" she tried.

Mr. Zulu shook his head, "No, Madam. This is the Tree of Forgetfulness. All the headmen here plant one of these trees in their village." Mr. Zulu held his forearm steady as if to demonstrate the power of the tree. "You can plant it just like that, from one stick, and it is so strong it will become a tree. They say ancestors stay inside it. If there is some sickness or if you are troubled by spirits, then you sit under the Tree of Forgetfulness and your ancestors will assist you with whatever is wrong." He nodded and took another drag of his cigarette. "It is true — all your troubles and arguments will be resolved."

"Do you believe that?" Mum asked, but before Mr. Zulu could reply she waved her own question away. "I believe it's true," she said. "I believe it two million percent."

Mum looked up into the branches of the tree again and she smiled. "Please bring me my camp chair, Mr. Zulu," she said. "I think I will have my tea here today." So Mr. Zulu went back to the truck to get Mum her chair. Dad, still weak from malaria, was lying under the tarpaulin watching the kettle boil over a mopane fire. "The madam has found the place for her house," Mr. Zulu reported. Dad propped himself up on an elbow and squinted in the direction of the river. Back-lit against the fierce afternoon sun, hands planted on her walking stick, was Mum — Nicola Fuller of Central Africa — mildly victorious under her Tree of Forgetfulness.

NICOLA FULLER OF CENTRAL AFRICA AT HOME

Mum and Dad, cocktail hour under the Tree of Forgetfulness. Zambia, 2010.

When I step off the airplane and into the Immigration and Customs Hall at Lusaka International Airport, Mum and Dad are waiting to greet me. They are standing in front of everyone else, pinned right up against the glass. Dad is in a blue town shirt, a pair of baggy Bermuda shorts, a pipe in his mouth. Mum is tipsy with excitement, in a pinstripe shirt and khaki pedal pushers. As soon as she sees me, she starts jumping up and down, and flashing her V for Victoria sign as if I am the first woman to fly solo across the Atlantic. "Whoo-hoo!" she hoots. "Whoo-hoo!"

But the closer I get to her, the less sure Mum is of what to do; she envelops me in a brief, uncomfortable embrace and tolerates a peck on the cheek. "Did they give you lots of yummy wine on the plane?" she asks. Dad — who has been looking mildly surprised since first glimpsing me (I have changed my hair color since the last time he saw me and while he can't put his finger on the difference, he knows there is one) — pummels my shoulders affectionately and takes my suitcase. "Bloody hell, Bobo," Dad says, and I know what he is about to say next — "How many pairs of shoes do you have in here?" — a persistent hangover from the time Mum took nothing but winklepickers and high-heel boots on their honeymoon to Tsavo National Park.

I am put in the bed of the pickup with an oil-bleeding generator, bags of fish food and my suitcase. "Are you sure you'll be okay back there, Bobo?" Mum asks, although she knows it's my preference.

"Fine," I say.

"Yes, it'll do her good after all that limousine treatment she's been getting over there," Dad says, patting the tailgate. He rolls down the window and pays the car guard. "Don't spend it all on wine and women," he advises, and then we're off, whistling through the perfect Lusaka night — the city sweetly pungent with the smell of diesel engines, burning rubbish, greening drains — sparks from Dad's pipe flying back around my shoulders and hair, for home.

At the top of my parents' garden at the fish and banana farm, there is a brick archway and wide brick steps leading past the Tree of Forgetfulness to an open-air kitchen where Big H spends her mornings preparing huge redolent stews of vegetables and cow bones for the dogs' supper, and her afternoons frowning over the supper Mum is preparing for the rest of us. "Ever since Big H got television and started watching those cooking shows, she has started to look down her nose at my curries," Mum says. Mum has always cooked whatever she can get her hands on: ropy chickens, mutton, crocodiles, frogs on the driveway — "They had deceptively promising thighs," Mum says — and turned them into fragrantly wonderful meals. "Big H thinks you're supposed to swear and sweat and have tantrums like Jamie Oliver," Mum says. "Not my nice, calm wine-infused meals."

On one side of the kitchen is the wood-stove, its back to the garden; on the other, there is a small laboring fridge (in the heat it merely produces sweating butter or water-beaded bottles, nothing ever gets really cold). Behind Big H, on a shelf dedicated to their storage, are Mum's nine orange Le Creuset pots. Their bottoms are permanently blackened with the drippings of the hundreds of curries and stews that have been cooked in them over the years.

To the right of the archway is a building containing my parents' bedroom and Mum's library with her collection of videos (musicals and operas mostly as well as British period dramas and a few nice, soothing murders); her books; and her art supplies. The top shelves are cluttered with carvings, ornaments and the brutalized bronze cast of Wellington (now missing both stirrups and reins, like a victim of a grueling Pony Club exercise).

To the left of the archway there is a two-roomed cottage comprising the guest bedroom and Dad's office. It is a thatched, brick structure inclined to be porous to wildlife. I open the door and wait. Nothing launches itself at my ankles, so I make my way to the bed and sit down, feet drawn up onto the bed. Big H brings me a clean towel, then stands around surveying the place. "Frogs," she observes at last, and leaves. As my eyes become accustomed to the gloom, I see what she means. The place is smothered in large, foam-nesting tree frogs, white as alabaster. They are hanging from the mosquito net, glued to the walls, attached to the door, hopping across the floor. Later, I find that if I drink half a box of South African wine and take a sleeping pill, a frog will become attached to my cheek while I sleep and will stay there unnoticed until morning. "How lucky for you," Mum says. "You can write about that in one of your Awful Books."

Work on the farm begins at dawn, while it is still cool, and I awake to find it well under way. There's Mum marching up to her fish ponds with a walking stick and a collection of dogs in her wake. "Those kingfishers are very greedy and very naughty," she says, waving her walking stick at a hovering shape over one of her ponds. There's Dad striding down to inspect his bananas — "Thirty-four kgs for a first bunch!" he announces trium-

Bo barely keeping up with Dad on the farm. Zambia, 2010.

phantly. My parents' farm is a miracle of productivity, order and routine — measuring, feeding, pruning, weeding, weighing, packing.

From the camp, Dad's bananas appear as a green cathedral of leaves. In the early days of the farm, elephants would make their way onto the farm at night and raid the fruit, stripping leaves, crushing stems. "They make a terrific mess," Mum says. Dad would wake up and hear them ripping through his plantation. "Talk about selective hearing," Mum says. "He can't hear a word I say, but let an elephant harm a hair on the head of one of his bananas and Dad bolts out of bed." Dressed only in a Kenyan kakoi and his blue Bata slip-ons, he raced down to the field waving a torch, "Come on you buggers that's enough of that. Off you go, go on!" Until eventually sleep deprivation forced Dad to put up an electric fence. "So that put an end to the elephants' picnics," Mum says.

Mum has taught herself everything she can about farm-raised tilapia — even flying with Chad Mbewe, her fish-section manager, to Malaysia for conferences on the latest techniques. "We both nearly died of cold in the icy air-conditioning," Mum says. "You need a serious down jacket and a scarf. I came home with bronchitis." In ten years, she has become the premier producer of fingerlings in the country, perhaps even the region. Her fish are famous for their quality, their ability to gain weight and their remarkably unstressed conditions. "Everyone has to be very calm and nicely turned out around Mum's fish," Dad warns. "You know what she's like." And it's true; it's not enough for Mum's ponds to be efficient, they must also be pleasant for the fish *and* artistically pleasing, as if she is substituting her farmwork for something that in another time and place she might have painted (sheep and geese grazing mostly peacefully along the ponds' edges; reeds picturesquely clumped at the corners; baobab trees, serene and ancient as a backdrop).

By midmorning, farmwork has been ongoing for five hours. Mum and Dad come in for breakfast, a meal consisting of pots and pots of tea, a slice of toast and a modest bowl of corn porridge. Then Dad puts his hat back on his head and Mum grabs her walking stick and her binoculars and out they go again. "Details, details, details," Mum says. "The devil lives in the details." But by early afternoon, the heat drives everyone indoors or toward shade and we retire to our frog-infested rooms for a siesta.

After our siesta and more tea, my parents are back out on the farm, Dad trailing a fragrant pulse of smoke from his pipe, Mum's walking stick thumping the ground with every stride. The soil under the bananas is being sampled for effective microorganisms; the fingerlings in several of the ponds are being counted; the shepherds are beginning to bring the sheep in for the night. Then the air takes on a heavy golden quality and we walk along the boundary with the dogs to Breezers, the pub at the bottom of the farm, in time to watch the egrets come in from the Zambezi to roost.

Before it is quite dark — "You don't want to bump into a bloody hippo," Dad says — we meander back up to the Tree of Forgetfulness, agreeably drunk. Mr. Zulu, a couple of his wives and several of his children are sitting on their veranda as we pass. Mr. Zulu nods a greeting and we exchange brief pleasantries. "Good evening, Mr. Zulu." "Yes, Mr. Fuller." His dogs mock-charge our dogs, which provokes Isabelle and Attatruk (Mum's turkeys) into hysterical gobbling, and then Lightning begins to bray (Flash died of sleeping sickness a few years ago). "It's quite like the musicians of Bremen," Mum says happily.

Before supper — my parents take the last meal of the day late, like Europeans — Mum makes for her bath with a glass of wine. Dad and I pour ourselves a drink under the Tree of Forgetfulness and play a languid game of twos and eights. "It's not nearly as much fun without Van here to cheat," I say. The dogs split themselves among laps, beds and chairs across the camp and begin to lick themselves. From the bathroom we can hear Mum drowning out Luciano Pavarotti. "Ah! Il mio sol pensier sei tu, Tosca, sei tu!" There is the occasional plop of an inattentive gecko falling from the rafters in the kitchen, where Big H has made a dish of turmeric rice to go with Mum's fish curry bubbling gently in one of the Le Creuset pots. All is as domestically blissful as it can get.

Suddenly the three dogs in the guest cottage start a loud, hysterical chorus of barking. It's been years since I've heard that particular bark, but I recognize it instantly. I put my cards down and look at Dad. "That's a snake bark," I say.

Dad takes his pipe out of his mouth and cocks his head, listening. "Oh bloody hell, you're right," he says. He hurries up the steps and I follow, hoping to look supportive, while also trying to ensure that I don't get to the door first. Dad walks into the guesthouse. "Okay, Bobo," he says, putting up a hand. I look down. He has just stepped over a beautifully patterned snake with a diamond-shaped head, as thick as a strong man's forearm — a puff adder. Puff adders kill more people than any other snake on the continent; their preferred diet is rodents and frogs (of which the Tree of Forgetfulness is an endlessly, self-replenishing buffet) and they strike from an S position so that they can hit a target at almost any angle. This one is in an S position now.

"Fetch Emmanuel," Dad says.

"A manual?" I repeat, my mind racing with the possibilities — *The Care and Prevention of Snakebite,* perhaps; or *Where There Is No Doctor.*

"Yes," Dad says. "First house on your left as you leave the yard."

So with Mum still singing her opera — "Vittoria! Vittoria! L'alba vindice appar" — I run under the brick archway at the top of the camp and into the pitch-dark Zambezi Valley night yelling for Emmanuel like a crazed missionary, "Emmanuel! Emmanuel!" And it occurs to me that this could very well be our triple obituary: Dad bitten to death by a puff adder; Mum drowned drunk in the bath listening to Puccini; me fallen into the dark and raptured into heaven while yelling for the Messiah. I imagine Vanessa at our mass funeral saying, "Well, this is bloody typical, isn't it?"

But between them, Dad and Emmanuel manage to kill the snake — or as Dad says, "give it a fatal headache" — using one of the many stout walking sticks Mum has bought over the years from a deaf-mute carpenter in the village. "How can I say no to the poor man?" she says, by way of explaining why she has so many. "I'm almost his only customer." And by the time Mum comes out of the bath, refreshed and ready for another glass of wine, order has been restored to the Tree of Forgetfulness: Emmanuel has gone back to his house; the deceased puff adder is in an empty beer crate behind the kitchen; the dogs are back on chairs and laps; Dad is shuffling the cards for another round of twos and eights.

"There was a puff adder in the guest-house," I tell Mum.

Mum doesn't look suitably impressed. "Oh?" She shakes the box of wine. "How much of this have you drunk?"

"Most of it," I say.

"Oh Bobo, really!"

"But my nerves," I object. "They're in shreds."

Mum sighs. "One tiny little snake and you collapse." Then Mum notices the broken walking stick and her face falls. "Oh no, *that* really is too bad. You didn't break one of my deaf-mute walking sticks, did you?"

"Well, which would you rather?" I ask. "Your deaf-mute walking stick or me?"

"I'd rather have my walking stick in one piece," Mum says, scooping up one of the Jack Russells and nuzzling its ear. "Wouldn't I, Papa Doc?"

"Right, that's it," I say. "I'm going to write an Awful Book and this time it really will be about you."

Mum sits down under the Tree of Forget-fulness, Papa Doc on her lap. She looks at Dad. "Did you hear that, Tim?" she says, her lips twitching. "Bobo's going to write the sequel."

"Say again," Dad says.

"AWFUL BOOK!" Mum shouts. "BO-BO'S GOING TO WRITE ANOTHER ONE."

ACKNOWLEDGMENTS

Mum and Dad. Lake Kariba. Zambia, 2008.

I wish to acknowledge authors whose work was most informative in the course of writing this book: Caroline Elkins; Trevor Royle; Leonard Thompson; Tom Mangold and Jeff Goldberg; Meryl Nass; Peter Godwin and Ian Hancock; Paul Moorcraft and Peter McLaughlin; SGM Herbert A. Friedman (Ret).

Deepest thanks to my agent, Melanie Jackson, for support and encouragement and for knowing that I had this story in my bones.

And also to my editor, Ann Godoff, for unfailing patience, compassion and for guidance, one sentence at a time.

Thanks to Joan Blatt for above-and-beyond extreme friendship.

Thanks to Mo Blum for healing amounts of wine, basil oil and soup.

Thanks to Bryan Christy — the smartest person I know — for reading every word of this book and for always making my words sharper.

Thanks to Katie Pierce for talking and walking this book out of me; and for putting mind, body and soul back together when they fell apart.

Thanks to Susie Rauch to whom I could always retreat when I most needed intelligent life, or a walk with too many dogs (which may amount to the same thing).

Thanks to David Shlim, who figured out what was ailing me and fixed it, and for compassion and encouragement.

Thanks to Terry Tempest Williams for knowing this territory so well and without whom this would have been a much lonelier work.

Thanks to Robin Binckes for help with translations (any errors are my fault entirely) and to Piet Smit for help with translations and also for reminding me that love of land is our African disease and our souls' cure.

Thanks to Carly Suek and Katie Thomas for providing a crucial pillar of support. Also thanks to Kate Healy.

Thanks to Melanie Schnizlein who quietly and calmly restored my home to tranquility so that I could write.

Thanks to my beloved Auntie Glug and Uncle Sandy for love and support and for all those days and nights in the nursery-comfort of Langlands.

Thanks to my sister, Vanessa Fuller Wootton-Woolley, for unflagging love, for protection and support, and for knowing.

Thanks to my children, without whom I would be lost: Sarah, for picking up the pieces and for providing endless humor and inspiration; Fuller, for abiding wit and kindness, for plates of scrambled eggs, for cups of tea; Cecily, for her sustaining lightness of being.

Thanks to my husband, Charlie, for forbearance and love.

But above all and always, I am indebted to my matchless and wonderful parents — Nicola and Tim Fuller — for their resilience, their humor, their compassion, their example and their generosity.

APPENDIX
NICOLA FULLER OF CENTRAL AFRICA: THE SOUNDTRACK

Mum with Papa Doc and Le Creuset pots.
Zambia, 2010.

"Come Fly with Me" — Frank Sinatra

"The Skye Boat Song" — Robert Louis Stevenson

"Fly Me to the Moon" — Frank Sinatra

"The Bandit" — Cliff Richard and The Shadows

"I Never Promised You a Rose Garden" —

Joe South (Lynn Anderson)

"From Russia with Love" — Matt Munro

"Sentimental Journey" — Doris Day

"God Save the Queen" — BBC Symphony Orchestra

"Shanghai" — Doris Day

William Blake's "Jerusalem" — BBC Symphony Orchestra

"Smoke Gets in Your Eyes" — The Platters

The Hallelujah Chorus from George Frideric Handel's *Messiah*

"The Banana Boat Song" — Harry Belafonte

"Everybody Loves My Baby" — Doris Day

"You Picked a Fine Time to Leave Me, Lucille" — Kenny Rogers

"The Last Farewell" — Roger Whittaker

"Dammi i colori . . . Recondita armonia," *Tosca* — Giacomo Puccini

GLOSSARY
A GUIDE TO UNUSUAL OR FOREIGN WORDS AND PHRASES

amore (Italian) — love

antbear (Oryceteropus afer) — aardvark

arrivderci (Italian) — good-bye

asante sana (Swahili) — thank you very much

ayah (Hindi) — children's maid

baas (Afrikaans) — boss

baobab (Adansonia digitata) — an enormous and iconic tree with a shiny bark reminiscent of elephant hide

batman — an officer's orderly or personal servant

boma — a chief's enclosure; a district government office

bywoner (Afrikaans) — sub-tenant or farm laborer; tenant farmer

cent' anni (Italian) — (may you live) a hundred years

choo (Swahili) — latrine (pronounced "cho"

as in "know")

che bello (Italian) — how beautiful

ciao, come stai? (Italian) — hello, how are you?

dit is jou perd (Afrikaans) — this is your horse

eucalyptus — see gum tree

fynbos — shrub land of mixed, hardy plants occurring in a small belt in the Western Cape

gum tree (*Eucalyptus bicostata*) — from the myrtle family, Myrtaceae, also known as eucalyptus. A diverse genus of flowering tree primarily originating in Australia but cultivated all over the tropics. The particular trees referred to here are commonly known as blue gums.

hadeda Ibis (Bostrychia hagedash) — a large dark brown ibis, common throughout much of east, central and south Africa

hensopper (Afrikaans) — someone who surrenders to, or joins, the enemy

high veldt — high plateau in southern Africa (cooler, wetter and generally more fertile and pleasant for human habitation than the low veldt)

hujambo askari (Swahili) — how are you, watchman?

huku (Shona) — chicken

il me nome e Nicola (Italian) — my name is Nicola

impala — a kind of antelope

kikoi (Swahili) — a brightly colored piece of cloth particular to East Africa, rather like a sarong

kirima kia ngoma (Swahili) — the place of devils

kloof (Afrikaans) — ravine, canyon

kom (Afrikaans) — come, let's go

kraal (Afrikaans) — livestock enclosure

lekker (Afrikaans) — nice

low veldt — lower elevations in southern Africa (hotter and drier and generally less fertile than high veldt)

maiwe (Shona) — my goodness!

miombo (Swahili) — see also msasa. Miombo refers to the woodland of brachystegia, a genus of tree comprising a large number of species. Typically, the bark of these trees is dark, their foliage is a feathery plume, shed during the dry season. New gold and red leaves are produced just before the onset of the rains. The tree is under threat as it is used extensively in the making of charcoal.

mopane (Colophospermum mopane) — grows in hot, low-lying areas, usually in so-called mopane woodlands

msasa (Brachystegia spiciformis) — see miombo

muli bwanje. Dzina landa ndine Nicola Fuller of Central Africa (Chinyanja) — Hello. My name is Nicola Fuller of Central Africa

munts — derogatory slang for black Zimbabweans (from muntu the Shona word meaning person)

mzuri sana (Swahili) — very good

nee dankie (Afrikaans) — no thank you

nile monitor (Varanus niloticus) — a large, highly-aquatic carnivorous lizard

nshima (Chinyanja) — see sadza. The staple of Zambia; a thick porridge made from corn.

nursing home — in the United States, a nursing home is predominantly for elderly residents but in England a nursing home is a maternity clinic or hospital

nyoka (Shona) — snake

op jou merke (Afrikaans) — on your marks

op Violet (Afrikaans) — here's to Violet

pamodzi (Chinyanja) — together

pole sana (Swahili) — very sorry

(the) Proms — formally known as the BBC Proms, or the Henry Wood Promenade Concerts presented by the BBC, the Proms is an eight-week summer season of daily classical music concerts held annually, predominantly in the Royal Albert Hall in London

povo — poor or impoverished people

pseudo ops — pseudo operations; black Rhodesian soldiers fighting for the Rhodesian government who infiltrated the ranks of guerilla (or freedom) fighters

pukka (Hindi) — superior, first-class; proper authentic

reedbuck — a species of antelope

sadza (Shona) — see also nshima. The food staple of Zimbabwe; a thick porridge made out of corn.

sahib/memsahib (Hindi) — master/mistress (used formerly as a respectful form of address for a European man/woman in India)

salwar kameez — a unisex dress of pants and a tunic worn in South and Central Asia

shamba (Swahili) — small plot or market

garden. After independence in Kenya, shambas were cut from larger, commercial farms and distributed among landless indigenous Kenyans.

shateen — bush, backcountry

sorry cloth — strips of very cheap, black cotton in which poor southern and central Africans bury their dead

syce (Hindi) — groom

terrs — slang for terrorists

trekboer (Afrikaans) — South African semi-nomadic pastoralists, primarily of Dutch descent

trekker (Afrikaans) — South African, primarily Afrikaner. The name refers to those who moved, usually from real or perceived persecution, from one European-settled area into areas not yet settled by Europeans.

Ugandan kob — type of antelope

veldskoen (Afrikaans) — literally "bush skin." The hide of animals made into leather hats and shoes.

veldt (Afrikaans) — grassland

voetsek (Afrikaans) — go away!

voortrekker (Afrikaans) — literally, "those who trek ahead." Afrikaners emigrants who moved into the South African interior in the 1830s and 1840s.

wattle — a genus of shrubs and trees belonging to the subfamily Mimosideae of the family Fabaceae. The bark of several species is rich in tannin used in the tanning of leather.

Wie get es dir? (German) — how are you?

zikomo kwambili (Chinyanja) — thank you very much

ABOUT THE AUTHOR

Alexandra Fuller was born in England in 1969 and in 1972 she moved with her family to a farm in Rhodesia. After that country's civil war in 1981, the Fullers moved first to Malawi, then to Zambia. Fuller received a B.A. from Acadia University in Nova Scotia, Canada. She is the author of *Don't Let's Go to the Dogs Tonight: An African Childhood,* a national bestseller, a *New York Times* Notable Book of 2002, and a finalist for the Guardian First Book Award, and *Scribbling the Cat,* winner of the 2005 Ulysses Award for Art of Reportage. Fuller lives in Wyoming with her husband and children.